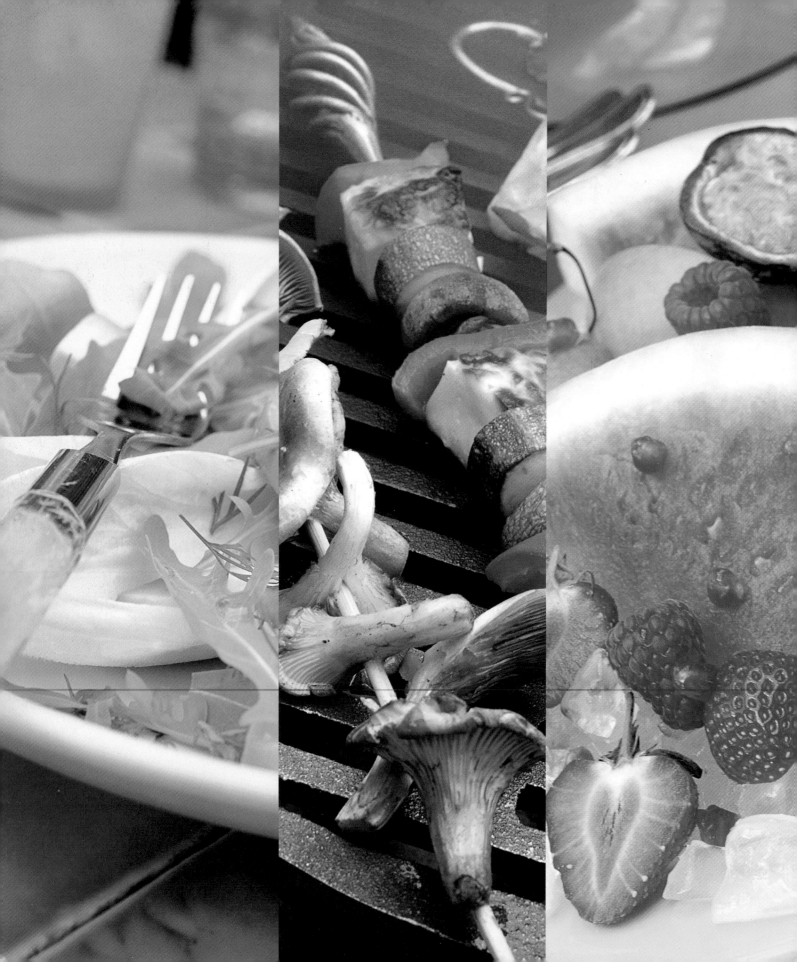

Acknowledgements

Many people have helped in the production of this book and I would like to thank them all, especially Polly Powell and Barbara Dixon for giving me the opportunity to write it, and my agent, Barbara Levy, for arranging the contract; Martin Ashton-Key who was responsible for the inclusion of the drinks section and supplied most of the recipes and a large part of the text for it; Chryssa Porter for her kindness and for the loan of both garden and (charcoal-burning) barbecue; Ann Weber (and David Brown) for many kind acts of friendship; Judy Ridgway for expert advice on olive oils; Mari Roberts for editing with such good humour and efficiency and being able to read both my mind and my handwriting; Anthony for realizing that a gas barbecue is a 'must' for serious recipe-testing and for buying me one; Claire for (her usual) great support and for keeping me down to earth; Clare Baggaley for inspired design and being such a pleasure to work with; Linda Burgess for her magic gift of seeing beauty in the simplest objects and for taking such inspiring photographs, and her daughter Jasmine for working so hard at the photo shoots; Sue Hutchings for preparing the recipes so well for the photos (and Vicky and Vanessa for helping in the kitchen), and Susan Bosanko for the index. My warmest thanks and appreciation to them all.

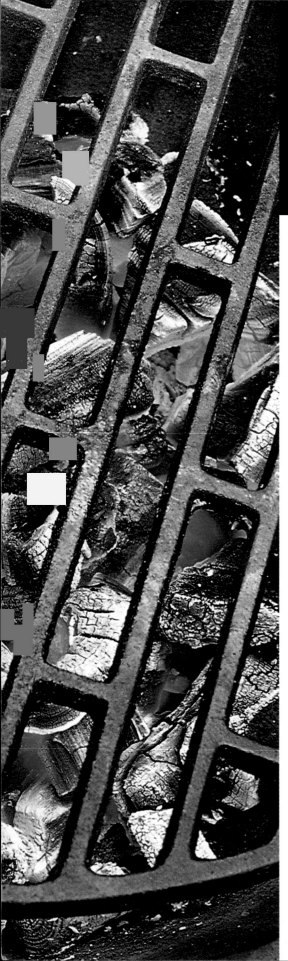

Contents

introduction

the food

A (V) *against a recipe indicates a vegan dish*

Introduction

When I started writing vegetarian cookery books, the first question I was invariably asked was: **'What <u>do</u> vegetarians eat for Christmas dinner?'** Now people ask: **'What <u>do</u> vegetarians eat at barbecues?',** and so I knew the time had come to write a book showing exactly that – vegetarian barbecues and grills, and how to make them.

One of the pleasures of barbecuing, apart from the **freedom and the open air,** is the sociability. Instead of being tucked away in the kitchen, the cook is at the centre of the party; and because the cooking and eating are going on simultaneously in a relaxed way, everyone feels involved. This spirit of friendly participation, which extended from the garden into this book, made this a highly enjoyable writing experience. Friends and family passed on their tips and recipes, cooked meals for me, lent me their barbecues so that I could test the recipes on different types of equipment, and even, in one case, brought me back a table-top model from Australia.

Experimental dishes were tasted enthusiastically. I was interested in the reaction of my meat-eating friends, and they said they found vegetarian food cooked in this way really satisfying, with no sense of 'something missing'. While I don't share the view that a meal without meat or fish is incomplete – on the contrary – I was interested in this. It might be our caveman (or cave-person) instincts: we associate the taste and smell of food cooked over an open fire with **fullness and satisfaction.** Eating in an informal way, out of doors and often with the hands, may also awaken atavistic memories.

More and more of my meals are now prepared in this way: outdoors on the barbecue in the summer, inside under the grill in the winter or when I'm in London. I hope you'll enjoy the recipes as much as I and my friends and family do.

What do vegetarians

Barbecue Equipment

All barbecues, whether the latest all-singing-all-dancing model, a version of your own construction with a grid balanced, say, on stones over a fire on the beach, or something in between, are essentially the same: a grid suspended over a heat source. There are different ways of providing the heat source and a variety of designs for the grid and its numerous attachments, so when buying a barbecue you need to consider what you want.

The first choice is between a barbecue that burns coals and one that is heated by gas or electricity. Gas and electric barbecues are quick, easy and convenient and ready for use almost at the touch of a button – they heat up in 10 to 15 minutes. They are easy to regulate and can be used for a long cooking period. A gas barbecue uses bottled gas: butane in summer, and in the winter, propane, which flows better at a colder temperature. Whereas a gas barbecue can be reasonably mobile, an electric one has, obviously, to be used within reach of a power point. Charcoal barbecues come in different designs, and these are covered below.

Other factors to bear in mind are whether your barbecue will be for frequent or occasional use, how many people you will be cooking for, and where you will use it and store it.

As with most things, you get what you pay for, and it's worth getting the best quality you can afford. In particular look for a barbecue that gives you enough cooking space on the grid for your requirements, and has bars that are not too far apart. Thicker bars are an advantage, too, because they give more 'browning' area on the food. I recommend buying a barbecue that has a cover which can be used over all or part of the grid to create a kind of oven. This gives more versatility and scope for cooking interesting dishes. Make sure that all handles are made from a material that will not get hot: wood or heat-treated plastic, for instance.

Each type of charcoal barbecue has its advantages and its devotees. The most popular are:

Covered kettles: round barbecues with lids – kettle-shaped, in fact. The sides reflect back heat all round for even cooking. These barbecues range in size from small, table-top models to large, free-standing ones on wheels. Excellent for most types of barbecue cooking.

Hooded barbecues: these are rectangular in shape, on rolling trolleys and used with or without lids. They often include extras such as rotisseries and movable grates.

Barrel and pedestal barbecues: shaped as their names suggest, the advantage of these is that their shape makes them easy to light and quick to heat up, so that they are ready for cooking in 10 to 15 minutes instead of the usual 45.

Do-it-yourself brick barbecues: available in kit form, these are an attractive proposition if you have the space and do not want a movable barbecue. You can create a large grilling area to suit your needs.

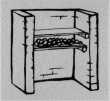

Disposable barbecues: these consist of a grid over a strong foil tray filled with charcoal and lighter, and I have found them surprisingly good. They are great for occasional use, for picnics, or where space is restricted such as on balconies or tiny patios.

eat at barbecues?

Types of charcoal

There are two types of charcoal: lumpwood and briquette. Lumpwood charcoal is made from wood heated in a kiln; briquettes are made by mixing charcoal waste with starch. Briquettes burn for longer than lumpwood charcoal. You can also buy 'instant' charcoal, which is impregnated with lighting fuel. It is becoming increasingly widely available and makes lighting the barbecue easy: simply put the instant charcoal in its bag into the barbecue tray and ignite the bag. Once it is burning, rake the coals level. You can always top up with more coal if necessary. Whichever type you choose, best results are obtained by using a good quality charcoal.

Preparing and lighting the fire

Begin about an hour before you want to start cooking because, unless you have a fast-heating barbecue, the coals take at least 45 minutes to heat up. Remove the lid of the barbecue and open all the vents. Make a bed of coals two layers deep: this will give you a fire for 45 to 60 minutes of cooking. For longer cooking, you will need to add more coals – see below. Don't make your fire any deeper at the start because it will be too hot to use.

To light the fire you can use kindling, fire-lighter sticks, gels or fluid; or an electric starter or a fire chimney.

Use a taper or a long match to apply the flame when the fuel is set, especially when using fire-lighting gel or fluid.

To use kindling, roll a sheet of newspaper tightly into a tube then bend it into a V shape. Put several of these V-shaped newspaper sticks into the bottom of the fuel grate, then arrange twigs, sticks and evenly shaped pieces of wood on top. On top of this build a pyramid of coals with air between them. Light the paper and, as the fire grows, add more coals. When the coals are hot, spread them out to make an even bed.

If you want to use fire-lighters, buy the kind that are specially made for barbecues. Build your coals into a pyramid shape, push in the fire-lighter sticks or blocks, and light.

If you are using a fluid starter – the most popular – pour a little on to the dry fuel, leave it to soak for a couple of minutes or so, then light it. Gel is squeezed on to the coals and lit. Put fluid or gel away once you have used it and be careful not to get any on to your hands because it could catch light and burn you . Never squirt lighter fluid on to a fire that is already burning – it could flare up and ignite the bottle in an instant.

An electric starter is a small oval heating element attached to a long handle with a cord. You put the element into the coals and the plug into an electric socket. The element heats up and sets fire to the coals. Once the coals are burning you simply remove the starter, putting it in a safe place. It is an easy and efficient way of igniting the fire if you have a power point near by.

A fire chimney is a tall metal chimney with air holes and handle. You remove the cooking grid from the barbecue and put the chimney in the grate. Put some crumpled newspaper into the bottom of the chimney then put coals on top – usually 45 to 50 – and light the paper. Once the coals are well alight carefully empty them into the grate.

Oil the grid before you start cooking to prevent food sticking to it.

Temperature guide

You need to wait until the flames are no longer licking round the coals and are beginning to form a light layer of ash. This usually takes about 45 minutes. The temperature is as follows:

HOT: the coals are red and glowing with ash beginning to form. You can hold your hand 15cm/6 inches above the cooking grid for about 2 seconds. Food can be quickly seared on the grid then pushed to the sides to cook through.

MEDIUM: the layer of ash is thicker with just an occasional red glow. You can hold your hand 15cm/6 inches above the grid for about 5 seconds. This temperature is suitable for most cooking.

COOL: the coals have a thick layer of ash and virtually no red glow. You can hold your hand over the grid for about 8 seconds. This temperature is good for slow-cooking foods such as fruits.

The fire burns hotter when the grate is open, without a lid, because of the effect of air on the coals. You can sear the outside of the food first then either move the food to the sides of the grid to cook more slowly right through, or cover with a lid, which reduces the heat of the fire by cutting down on the amount of air getting to it.

You can control the cooking heat by moving the grid closer to (or further from) the coals. Tapping the coals with tongs to knock off some of the ash will also raise the heat a little, as will opening the vents or removing the lid. Conversely, to cool the fire, spread the coals out using tongs, or half-close any vents.

If you want to cook for longer than 45 to 60 minutes, you will need to add more coals. Put them around the edges of the fire to heat up, or light more coals in a second barbecue or large roasting tin and add them to the grate when hot.

Dealing with flare-ups

If you get a 'flare-up', caused by oil dripping off the food into the fire, simply aim a narrow jet of water from a spray bottle (kept for this purpose) directly at the source of the flame. It will subside immediately. I have even put out flare-ups with a squirt of juice from half a lemon.

Putting out the fire and cleaning up

When you have finished cooking, close the vents and cover the barbecue with a lid if it has one. If you have cooked on an open fire, spray the coals with water. Unburnt charcoal can be saved for future use but mix it with new coal as it takes longer to light and doesn't burn as hot. Let the barbecue cool down completely – this can take several hours – before dismantling, cleaning and storing it. When the rack is cold, scrub it with a wire brush then wash it with a soap-filled scouring pad. If a lot of food is burnt on to it, use an oven-cleaner.

If you have a gas barbecue, clean the rack, burners and drip trays before packing it away.

Safety Guidelines

1 Follow the manufacturer's directions for assembling and using the barbecue.

2 Position the barbecue on a level surface away from the house, and away from dry leaves or anything that could catch fire. Put portable barbecues on a heatproof surface.

3 Don't barbecue when the weather is very windy.

4 Never use a barbecue indoors unless it has been designed for this purpose.

5 Always open the lid of a gas barbecue before lighting and never use charcoal on a gas barbecue.

6 Never squirt petrol or lighter fluid into the fire; it can flare up and set you alight. Use liquid starter only before the fire has been lit and then put it away in a safe, cool place.

7 Keep matches away from the barbecue once it's alight.

8 Never leave a barbecue unattended; have everything you need close by before you start so you don't have to keep going into the house.

9 Watch children and pets carefully; keep them away from the barbecue.

10 Use long-handled cooking tools and don't wear loose clothes with floppy sleeves.

11 When opening the lid of the barbecue, do so carefully away from you and anybody else, to avoid being burned by the steam and smoke.

12 Don't move the barbecue once it's alight.

13 Never try to put out the fire by pouring water on it. This could cause the metal of the barbecue to contract too quickly and crack. Let it cool completely before cleaning it and putting away – this can take several hours.

Cooking Tools

Essentials are long-handled tongs, a fish slice or spatula for turning food, a long-handled brush for basting, a pair of oven gloves and a spray bottle for squirting water at flare-ups. I also consider essential a fine-mesh rack that rests on the normal grid and enables you to cook smaller pieces of food that would otherwise fall through the bars. A non-stick baking tray that fits the top of the barbecue is useful, too, but I don't use this nearly as much as the fine-mesh grid, which I keep permanently on the barbecue.

A set of flat metal skewers and a packet of bamboo or wooden skewers give further recipe options. You might like to consider buying a hinged wire rack for holding several burgers, enabling you to turn them easily – but I prefer to turn them individually with tongs or a fish slice. A wire brush is handy for cleaning the rack when food gets stuck to it.

It's useful to have a table near the barbecue so that you can lay out your tools, dishes and ingredients and do simple last-minute preparation; a rubbish bin and a damp cloth nearby complete the line-up.

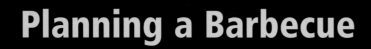

Planning a Barbecue

One of the things that makes barbecuing enjoyable is that so much of the preparation can be done in advance, leaving you free to concentrate on the cooking and the company.

A barbecued meal usually consists of main dishes that are cooked outdoors and accompaniments that are either uncooked or cooked indoors. A main vegetable dish and some halloumi cheese or burgers cooked on the barbecue, served with a sauce, salsa or creamy dip, a salad and warm bread, for instance, would make a good array.

Accompaniments can be prepared in advance and kept in a cool place to bring outside or reheat in the oven at the last minute. Vegetables can be left to marinate; burgers, cheese or whatever else you are having can be prepared ready for grilling. As the embers cool, puddings can be cooked on the barbecue, supplemented with sauces and ice creams made or bought in advance. When planning what to cook I tend to take dishes which come roughly from one country or area; that way you can create mouth-watering menus. Here are some suggestions, taken from this book:

Thai Aubergine in Coconut Marinade, page 52; Marinated Tofu Kebabs, page 45, with Oriental Rice Noodle Salad, page 96; Thai Sweetcorn Fritters, page 78 and Red Chilli Sauce, page 112; Peaches in White Wine, page 127; Yogurt Cinnamon Cream, page 130.

Tandoori Potato Skewers, page 47, with Spiced Rice Salad with Nuts and Seeds, page 97; Nan Bread cooked on the barbecue, page 39; Whole Garlic Grilled with Rosemary, page 61; Open Mushrooms with Red Pepper Pesto, page 62; Mixed Tomato Salad, page 99; Yogurt and Herb Sauce, page 107; Grilled Peaches, page 127; Passion Fruit Cream, page 130.

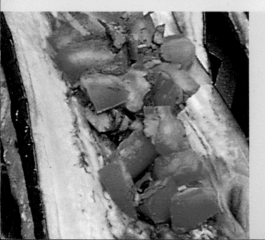

Chunky Chips of Sweet Potatoes with Chilli-Lime Marinade, page 67; Soured Cream Dip, page 29; Grilled Sweetcorn, see Three Ways with Sweetcorn, page 70; Peanut Burgers, page 76, with Coriander Salsa, page 110, and Easy Crunchy Coleslaw, page 99; Grilled Pineapple with Brown Sugar and Rum, page 125; Coconut and Lime Cream Topping, page 130.

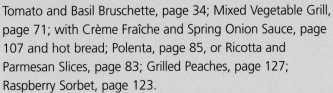
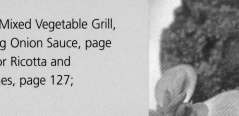

Tomato and Basil Bruschette, page 34; Mixed Vegetable Grill, page 71; with Crème Fraîche and Spring Onion Sauce, page 107 and hot bread; Polenta, page 85, or Ricotta and Parmesan Slices, page 83; Grilled Peaches, page 127; Raspberry Sorbet, page 123.

Garlic Mushroom Skewers, page 43, with hot bread; Goat's Cheese Burgers, page 75, with Apricot and Lemon Sauce, page 112; Garlic Potato Wedges, page 66; Courgettes in Yogurt and Mint Marinade with Crème Fraîche and Dill, page 60; Frisée Salad with Croûtons, page 89; Grilled Chocolate Bananas, page 125; Quick and Easy Ice Cream, page 120.

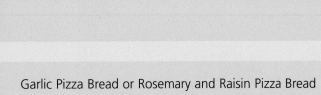
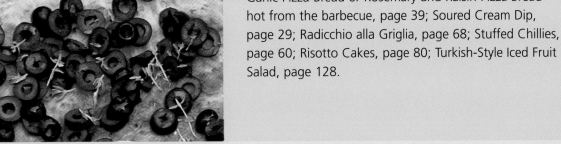

Garlic Pizza Bread or Rosemary and Raisin Pizza Bread hot from the barbecue, page 39; Soured Cream Dip, page 29; Radicchio alla Griglia, page 68; Stuffed Chillies, page 60; Risotto Cakes, page 80; Turkish-Style Iced Fruit Salad, page 128.

Grilled Asparagus with Lemon and Pepper Marinade, page 51, with Quick Hollandaise Sauce, page 117; Gnocchi alla Romana, page 84, with Soured Cream Dip, page 29; Golden Peppers Stuffed with Peperonata, page 102; Basil Salad, page 89; Grilled Peaches, page 127; Instant Strawberry Ice Cream, page 121.

Asparagus and Oyster Mushroom Kebabs, page 47; Tomato and Cheese Pizza, page 38; Salad of Chicory, Fresh Dill, Wild Rocket and Avocado, page 100; Grilled Chocolate Bananas, page 125 ; Grilled Peaches, page 127, with Butterscotch Sauce, page 131; Coconut Ice Cream, page 120.

Marinades, Pastes and Butters

Marinades – mixtures of liquids and flavourings in which ingredients are steeped before cooking – have traditionally been used to **tenderize and flavour meat and fish**. However, I have discovered that **marinades are emphatically not just for meat**, although the role they play in vegetable cookery is a little different.

A marinade will not penetrate most vegetables as it does meat; the effect is more superficial. Flavour is imparted to the surface, so the way the vegetable is cut is important. As vegetables contain no fat, the oil in the marinade is necessary to prevent them from sticking to the grill. Excess marinade can be used for **basting** or in a **sauce**, as in a number of recipes in this book; or it can be kept in the refrigerator for a day or so and used again. Most vegetables will absorb **maximum flavour** in about 30 to 60 minutes (occasionally longer) so the process is much quicker than with meats, which may take up to 24 hours.

A marinade usually consists of an acidic base such as wine, vinegar, citrus juice, yogurt, soy sauce or mustard, and oil with herbs and spices. A touch of **honey** or **sugar** is effective – but they burn easily so are used in small quantities. **Sea salt** is generally added after the marinating process.

Ordinary **vin de table** is generally all that is required. **Dry vermouth** can also be effective. I've not managed to marinate vegetables in beer: the flavour is too crude.

The type of **olive oil** you use has a subtle but definite effect on the flavour of the finished dish. If you have the time and inclination, experiment with oils from different countries. French oils are rather too delicate for barbecuing; more **robust oils**, such as those from Greece, Spain and Italy, are needed. The ideal would be to match the oil to the 'nationality' of the ingredients. For a marinade with Italian ingredients, for instance, use an Italian olive oil. This is a counsel of perfection – any good all-purpose **virgin olive oil** which is robust enough to stand up to the other flavourings is fine, and Greek olive oils are often a good choice. In America, choose an olive oil from an estate using European varieties.

A marinade is most effective when the ingredients are at room temperature or even slightly warm. The marinade can be made an hour or so before use, to allow the flavours to develop. The **vegetables** need to be put in a single layer in a

shallow dish or tin (not aluminium). The marinade is then poured over them. You do not need to submerge them but make sure there's enough liquid to come up round the edges. **Turn the vegetables over from time to time to ensure complete and even coverage.** Another, neat way to marinate is to put the vegetables and marinade into a **polythene bag**. Close the top; the ingredients can be moved around in the bag, and the bag can be discarded after use.

When barbecuing marinated vegetables, let the marinade run off them first. Save it for **lightly brushing** them during cooking and for pouring over them when cooked. Excess marinade dripping off the vegetables will burn on the coals and perhaps cause flare-up.

Also here are recipes for **pastes** and **flavoured butters**. **Pastes** give partially cooked vegetables a **tasty coating**. **Flavoured butters** melt and impart both **flavour** and **moisture** to simply grilled vegetables.

Italian Red Wine Marinade (v)

This marinade is excellent with artichokes, chicory and large open mushrooms.

ingredients

300ml / 10fl oz dry red Italian
table wine

4 tablespoons olive oil

6 garlic cloves, crushed

3–4 sprigs of fresh thyme

4 bay leaves

coarse sea salt and freshly
ground black pepper, to taste

Mix all the ingredients together well.

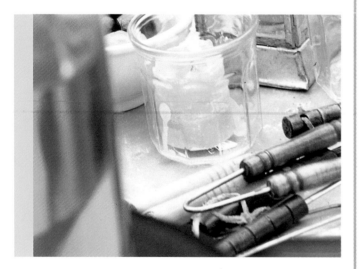

Spanish Red Wine Marinade (v)

Although I usually prefer to use fresh garlic, I used the purée (it comes in jars and tubes) for a shortcut when I was testing recipes for this book and was surprised to find it perfectly satisfactory for recipes such as this. This marinade is superb with artichokes, as well as shallots, onions and leeks.

ingredients

300ml / 10fl oz medium-dry red Spanish
table wine

4 tablespoons olive oil

generous sprigs of fresh thyme

2 good-sized bay leaves

2 tablespoons garlic purée

3 tablespoons tomato purée

Mix all the ingredients together well.

White Wine and Tarragon Mustard Marinade (V)

ingredients

300ml / 10fl oz medium-dry white *vin de pays*

4 tablespoons olive oil

7 tablespoons green mustard with tarragon

3 tablespoons chopped fresh tarragon

1 tablespoon dried sage

Tarragon mustard, the flavour reinforced with some chopped fresh tarragon and some dried sage, gives this marinade its zing.

Mix all the ingredients together well.

Vermouth and Juniper Marinade (V)

ingredients

4 tablespoons dry white vermouth or martini

200ml / 7fl oz dry white wine

juice of 1 lemon

3 tablespoons olive oil

1 tablespoon crushed juniper berries

½ small onion, finely chopped

¼ teaspoon ground black pepper

Mix all the ingredients together well.

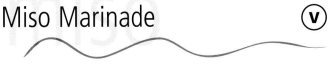

Miso Marinade (V)

This marinade gives a Japanese flavour to grilled vegetables; it's especially delicious with baby aubergines (see page 55). There are various types of miso; a light one is the best for this recipe. I like Amakuchi Barley and Soy Mugi, organic unpasteurized miso. Once bought, it keeps for months in the refrigerator. You can buy this particular miso from Clearspring in London, which has a mail-order service, though I expect you could get something similar (though perhaps not organic and unpasteurized) from an Asian grocer or a health-food shop.

ingredients

50g / 2oz light miso paste

1 tablespoon light brown sugar

2 tablespoons sherry

Mix all the ingredients together well.

Lemon and Olive Oil Marinade (V)

Quick and simple, this enhances most vegetables.

ingredients

6 tablespoons olive oil

1–2 garlic cloves, crushed

juice of 3 lemons

freshly ground black pepper, to taste

Mix all the ingredients together well.

Variations

Lemon and Garlic Marinade (V)

Increase the quantity of garlic to 6–8 cloves.

Lemon and Wholegrain Mustard Marinade (V)

Add 2 heaped tablespoons wholegrain mustard to the marinade.

Chilli-Lime Marinade (V)

ingredients

juice of 4 limes

6 tablespoons olive oil

1 green chilli, seeded and sliced, or chilli powder to taste

1 tablespoon chopped fresh coriander

1 teaspoon cayenne pepper

Mix all the ingredients together well.

Lemon and Pepper Marinade (V)

One of my favourite marinades: the freshness of the lemon and the zing of the peppercorns enhance many vegetables. For coarsely ground black peppercorns you can use a pestle and mortar, though easier, and just as effective in my opinion, is to buy a jar of coarsely ground black pepper (sometimes called steak pepper).

ingredients

6 tablespoons olive oil

grated rind and juice of 1 lemon

1 garlic clove, crushed

½ teaspoon sea salt

1 bay leaf, torn in half

1 teaspoon coarsely ground black peppercorns

6 tablespoons white wine, optional

Mix all the ingredients together well, including the wine if using.

Left to right: Raspberry Vinegar Marinade (page 23) and Lemon and Olive Oil Marinade

Tomato and Lemon Marinade (v)

ingredients

juice of ½ lemon

6 tablespoons olive oil

300ml / 10fl oz passata

4 garlic cloves, crushed

freshly ground black pepper, to taste

This is excellent with chicory.

Mix all the ingredients together well.

Yogurt and Mint Marinade

ingredients

300ml / 10fl oz plain yogurt

3 tablespoons light olive oil

2 garlic cloves, crushed

juice of ½ lemon

2 tablespoons chopped fresh mint

Mix all the ingredients together well.

Greek Tomato Marinade (v)

ingredients

6 garlic cloves, crushed

2 heaped tablespoons Greek tomato purée

2 heaped tablespoons Italian dried herbs

6 tablespoons olive oil

juice of 1 lemon

freshly ground black pepper, to taste

A Greek tomato purée I found in a Greek Cypriot shop was the inspiration for this marinade. However, an ordinary tomato purée will do if you cannot get the Greek one.

Mix all the ingredients together well.

Thai Coconut Marinade

ingredients

1 tablespoon ground coriander

2 green chillies, seeded and finely sliced

grated rind and juice of 1 lime

1 lemongrass stalk – discard any tough outer layers and finely chop the rest

2 kaffir lime leaves, dried or fresh, finely shredded, optional

1 garlic clove, crushed

1 tablespoon light brown sugar

200ml / 7fl oz canned coconut milk

Put the ground coriander into a small saucepan and stir for a few seconds over the heat until the aroma is released – be careful not to burn it. Transfer the coriander to a bowl and add all the remaining ingredients, mixing together well.

Vinegar Marinades

Balsamic Vinegar Marinade ⓥ

ingredients

1 tablespoon soy sauce

3 tablespoons balsamic vinegar

4 tablespoons olive oil

1 large garlic clove, crushed

freshly ground black pepper, to taste

Put the soy sauce and vinegar into a bowl and mix together until combined; then stir in the olive oil, garlic and pepper.

Variations

Honey, Mustard and Balsamic Vinegar Marinade

Add a tablespoonful each of honey and Dijon mustard, mixing them with the soy sauce and vinegar before adding the oil. This makes a thick, sweet and tangy marinade. Makes ordinary supermarket mushrooms really interesting, gives depth of flavour to aubergines as well as making them very tender, and is superb with tofu.

Balsamic Vinegar, Honey and Thyme Marinade

Add 1 tablespoon honey and 2 teaspoons dried thyme, stirring them with the soy sauce and vinegar before adding the oil.

Balsamic Vinegar and Ginger Marinade ⓥ

Mix 1 tablespoon grated fresh ginger with the soy sauce and vinegar before adding the olive oil.

Sara's Marinade

ingredients

4 tablespoons tomato ketchup

2 tablespoons honey

4 garlic cloves, crushed

2 tablespoons olive oil

2 tablespoons soy sauce

1 tablespoon wine vinegar

My niece, Sara, an inspired cook, gave me this recipe for her very easy, sweet and tangy marinade.

Sweet and simple. Mix all the ingredients together well.

Raspberry Vinegar Marinade ⓥ

I used a raspberry vinegar which had whole raspberries still in the bottle. If this is unavailable you can use a strained one, and if the recipe calls for the strained raspberries, as in the radicchio recipe on page 68, just add a few fresh or frozen ones. (Illustrated on page 21.)

ingredients

6 tablespoons raspberry vinegar

2 tablespoons olive oil

grated rind of ½ lemon

sea salt and freshly ground black pepper, to taste

If necessary, strain the vinegar through a sieve to remove the whole raspberries – leave on one side to use later if required. Mix the vinegar with the rest of the ingredients, using just a pinch of sea salt and freshly ground black pepper.

Pastes

Tomato and Garlic Paste (V)

ingredients

6 garlic cloves, crushed, or
1 tablespoon garlic purée

1 tablespoon sun-dried tomato
paste

2 tablespoons tomato purée

1 tablespoon olive oil

sea salt and freshly ground black
pepper, to taste

Mix all the ingredients
together into a paste.

Tandoori Paste (V)

ingredients

2 garlic cloves, crushed

2 tablespoons ground cumin

2 tablespoons olive oil

juice of ½ lemon

sea salt and freshly ground black
pepper, to taste

Mix all the ingredients
together into a paste.

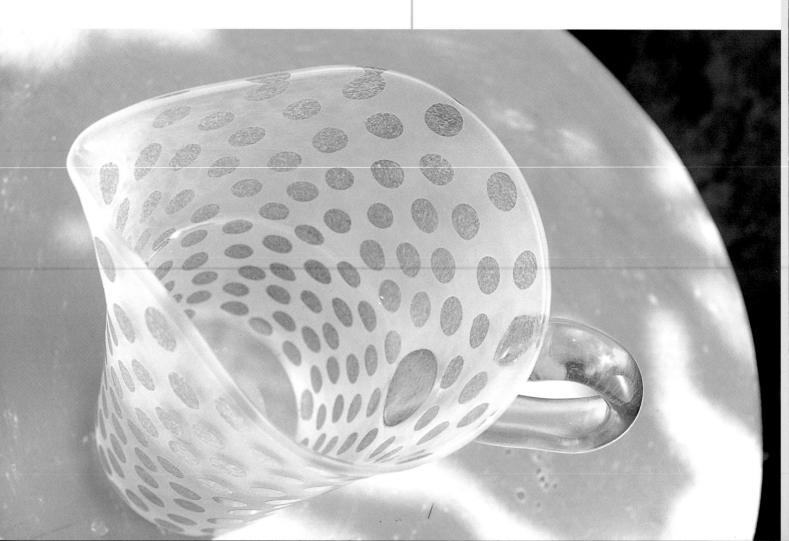

Butters

Flavoured Butter

ingredients

125g / 4oz lightly salted butter

flavourings as required

Beat the butter to soften it, then mix in your chosen flavourings. Form the butter into a sausage shape then wrap in clingfilm and chill until firm. Slice off rounds as required. Any remaining butter will keep in the refrigerator for up to 4 days, and in the freezer for up to 4 weeks. These butters are great for livening up plainly grilled vegetables: as the butter melts, it adds extra flavour and moisture.

Flavourings

Black Pepper and Lemon Butter

Crush 1 tablespoon black peppercorns using a pestle and mortar or buy coarsely ground black pepper (sometimes called steak pepper). Beat into the butter along with the finely grated zest of 1 lemon.

Green Peppercorn Butter

Crush 1 tablespoon dried green peppercorns in a pestle and mortar or mash 1 tablespoon drained green peppercorns preserved in brine. Beat into the butter.

Mixed Peppercorn Butter

For a pretty coloured butter which also tastes great, crush 1 tablespoon mixed peppercorns – red, white, green and black – and beat into the butter.

Red Chilli Butter

For this hot butter, crush 4 dried red chillies – an easy way to do this is to snip them finely with kitchen scissors – and mix them, seeds and all, into the butter with a good pinch of paprika.

Garlic and Herb Butter

An old favourite, best made really garlicky with 4 crushed fat garlic cloves and 1–2 tablespoons chopped fresh green herbs such as chives and parsley.

Juniper and Shallot Butter

Crush 1 tablespoon juniper berries in a pestle and mortar or on a board with the back of a wooden spoon, and mix into the butter along with 1–2 finely chopped shallots.

Dips,
Breads
and Pizzas

One of the secrets of a successful barbecue is to ensure everyone has something to eat and drink quickly. **Bruschette – delicious crisp breads** which you can make in minutes on the barbecue and top with tasty morsels – fit the bill perfectly.

Alternatively, you could serve one or two of these **dips and toppings** along with **crisps, tortilla chips** and **crudités**. Dips are versatile, quick to make and equally suitable as a dip or spooned over **barbecued vegetables, savoury cakes** or **burgers**.

If you're eating **crudités** with the dips, serve a good variety of vegetables, and avoid any that you will be grilling later. I particularly like **tender summer radishes,** just washed and with their green leaves still intact, **spring onions,** and, particularly effective as scoops, **cauliflower florets.**

Also in this section are recipes for **home-made pizzas and various breads.** It might seem a bit ambitious to make your own bread on the barbecue, but it's **surprisingly easy** and the results are superb, so I do urge you to give it a try. These breads are **quick to cook,** which makes them ideal for eating early on in the proceedings while the burgers and vegetables for the next course are cooking. You can **flavour the dough** with fresh or dried herbs, black and green olives, sun-dried tomatoes, walnuts or pine nuts, dried raisins or apricots ... **whatever you fancy,** really. A few of my favourite ways with barbecued breads are given on page 39, and on page 31, the barbecued breads are shown topped with sliced black olives and thyme, and with briefly fried red onions and fresh rosemary.

A couple of interesting cocktails or aperitifs as well as or instead of wine would also go down well: **alcoholic** and **non-alcoholic** recipes are on pages 132–41, together with some thoughts on **wines and beers** that go particularly well with grilled and barbecued food.

With a drink in one hand and **warm, fragrant bread** in the other, waiting for the feast to begin becomes a **pleasure.**

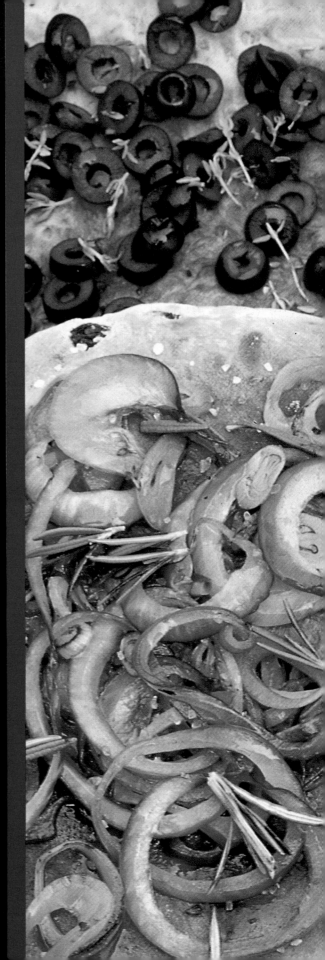

Artichoke Paste (v)

serves 2–4

This is good as a topping for a bruschetta or pizza, or as a filling for grilled peppers.

ingredients

425g / 15oz can artichoke hearts, drained

juice of ½ lemon

1 garlic clove, crushed

2 tablespoons olive oil

1 tablespoon roughly chopped fresh parsley

coarsely ground black pepper

Put the artichoke hearts into a food processor with the lemon juice, garlic, olive oil, parsley and pepper to taste, and blend to a purée – chunky or smooth according to your taste. Transfer to a small bowl to serve.

Gorgonzola Dip

serves 4

This is excellent made with Gorgonzola cheese, but you can also use other blue cheeses such as Stilton or Danish blue. It's a sharp-tasting, tangy dip, which contrasts well with the sweetness of marinated vegetables.

ingredients

200g / 7oz curd cheese or low-fat soft smooth white cheese

100g / 3½oz Gorgonzola cheese

a few drops of milk to moisten

sea salt and freshly ground black pepper

It's easiest to make this in a food processor, though you can make it by hand. Put the curd cheese or low-fat soft white cheese into a food processor or bowl. Crumble in the Gorgonzola, then process or beat until fairly smooth, adding a little milk if necessary for a soft consistency. Season with a little sea salt and a grinding of black pepper, transfer to a small bowl and serve.

Smoky Aubergine Dip

serves 4

The charring of the aubergine is ideally done over the grill or barbecue; it needs to get really black, then to cool before you cut it, scoop out the tender flesh within and blend to a cream with the other ingredients. In practical terms this means charring the aubergine one day, serving the purée another; or charring it under the grill indoors. Either way, the smoky taste and smooth texture are well worth the effort.

ingredients

2 large aubergines

3 garlic cloves, crushed

2 tablespoons freshly squeezed lemon juice

1 tablespoon olive oil

2 tablespoons Greek yogurt or tahini

sea salt and freshly ground black pepper

Put the whole aubergines over the coals or under a hot grill until they are soft and charred all over. Let them cool, then slit them open lengthways and scoop out the flesh, avoiding the charred skin. Put the flesh into a bowl or food processor with the garlic, lemon juice, oil and yogurt or tahini and mash well with a fork or process until creamy. Season with sea salt and pepper. Spoon into a small bowl to serve.

Soured Cream Dip

serves 4

ingredients

300ml / 10fl oz soured cream

2–3 tablespoons chopped fresh dill

sea salt and freshly ground black pepper, to taste

Mix all the ingredients together well. Spoon into a small bowl for dipping.

White Bean Dip ⓥ

serves 4–6

White beans prepared this way form a creamy and delicious purée.

ingredients

425g / 15oz can white beans such as cannellini or butter beans

2 garlic cloves

4 tablespoons freshly squeezed lemon juice

1 tablespoon olive oil

4–5 sprigs of fresh parsley, stalks removed

cayenne pepper or chilli powder

a few drops of red wine vinegar

sea salt and freshly ground black pepper

Drain the beans, saving the liquid. Put the beans into a food processor with the garlic and blend to a purée, making sure that the garlic gets well chopped. Then add the lemon juice, olive oil and parsley. Whiz again, to a smooth cream, adding some of the reserved bean liquid to get a soft consistency. Add a pinch or two of cayenne pepper or chilli powder and perhaps a few drops of red wine vinegar to give it a kick. Season to taste with sea salt and pepper and transfer to a small bowl to act as a dip.

Variation

Butter Bean and Black Olive Dip ⓥ

Make the dip with butter beans, then add 50–125g / 2–4oz stoned and chopped black olives. (Buy whole kalamata olives and stone them yourself for maximum flavour.)

Goat's Cheese and Herb Dip

serves 4

Use a plain, smooth, mild goat's cheese or, for a stronger flavoured dip, try a 'peppered' version.

ingredients

200g / 7oz soft white goat's cheese

1–2 tablespoons hot water

1 garlic clove, crushed

2–3 tablespoons chopped fresh parsley, chives, dill and/or oregano (use at least two)

pinch of chilli powder or cayenne pepper, optional

sea salt and freshly ground black pepper

Put the cheese into a bowl and stir in some of the hot water until you have a soft 'dipping' consistency. Mix in the garlic, herbs, chilli powder or cayenne, and sea salt and freshly ground black pepper to taste. Spoon into a small bowl to serve.

On the grid: Rosemary and Raisin Pizza Bread (page 39), topped with fried red onions and fresh rosemary; Cheese and Onion Pizza Bread (page 39), topped with olives and thyme, plus Whole Grilled Garlic with Rosemary (page 61). In the foreground: Butter Bean and Black Olive Dip and Goat's Cheese and Herb Dip

Hummus (V)

serves 4–6

Creamy hummus goes well with grills and barbecues. Although it's widely available from supermarkets, if you have a food processor it's better to make your own flavoured exactly to your taste.

ingredients

425g / 15oz can chickpeas

4–5 garlic cloves

1 tablespoon light tahini

4 tablespoons freshly squeezed lemon juice

1 tablespoon olive oil

sea salt and freshly ground black pepper

Drain the chickpeas, saving the liquid. Put the chickpeas into a food processor with the garlic and blend to a purée, making sure that the garlic gets well chopped. Then add the tahini, lemon juice and olive oil. Whiz again, to a smooth cream, adding some of the reserved liquid to get a soft, creamy consistency. Season with salt and pepper. Spoon into a bowl to serve.

Guacamole (V)

serves 4

Traditional guacamole is more like a salad or a salsa than a smooth dip. This goes particularly well with barbecued breads, vegetables and burgers.

ingredients

2 tomatoes, skinned

½–1 green chilli, seeded

¼ bunch fresh coriander

1 large ripe avocado

sea salt and freshly ground black pepper

Coarsely chop the tomatoes, chilli and coriander by hand or briefly whiz them in a food processor. Put this coarse purée into a bowl and leave in a cool place until just before you want to serve the guacamole.

At the last minute, cut the avocado in half, remove the stone and scoop out the flesh. Mash the flesh and add it to the other ingredients in the bowl, beating with a fork to combine well. Season with sea salt and pepper and serve at once.

Tsatsiki

serves 4

This makes a good appetizer, for nibbling while the food is cooking. It's also great as a sauce or topping for burgers, and is wonderful with hot crusty bread, perhaps straight off the barbecue.

ingredients

½ cucumber

sea salt

200g / 7oz carton Greek yogurt

1 garlic clove, crushed

2–3 tablespoons chopped fresh mint or dill

pinch of chilli powder or cayenne pepper, optional

freshly ground black pepper

Peel the cucumber and finely dice the flesh. Put the dice into a colander and sprinkle with sea salt. Cover with a plate and a weight to press them down, then leave them until just before you want to serve the tsatsiki.

To finish the tsatsiki, turn the cucumber out of the colander on to a double layer of kitchen paper and pat dry. Put the yogurt into a bowl and add the cucumber, garlic, chopped mint or dill, a pinch of chilli powder or cayenne to give it a bit of a kick if you wish, and some freshly ground black pepper. Stir gently to combine, then serve.

Tapenade

serves 4–6

This Provençal dip usually contains anchovies but you can make a very good vegetarian version flavoured with chilli, garlic and capers along with the black olives. For best results use good quality olives – I like kalamata – and stone them yourself.

ingredients

125g / 4oz stoned black olives

25g / 1oz drained capers

1 garlic clove

1 dried red chilli, crumbled or snipped

4 tablespoons olive oil

sea salt and freshly ground black pepper

Put the olives into a food processor with the capers, garlic and chilli and whiz until all the ingredients are well chopped. Then add the olive oil and whiz again. Season – you may not need sea salt because of the saltiness of the olives and capers.

Variation

Green Tapenade

Make tapenade as described, replacing the black olives with large green ones.

Tomato and Basil Bruschette ⓥ

serves 4

Bruschette make excellent, crunchy starters or accompaniments to grilled food and are easy to make. In Italy panne rustica would be used, but this bread is difficult to obtain here. I find a granary or wholewheat loaf makes a good substitute.

ingredients for the bruschette bases

4 slices of good bread

1 garlic clove, halved

olive oil for drizzling

FOR THE TOMATO AND BASIL TOPPING:

450g / 1lb tomatoes, skinned and chopped

salt and freshly ground black pepper

4 sprigs of fresh basil

Lay the slices of bread on the barbecue grid and toast each side – it will only take a minute or two. (You can also toast them under a hot grill.) Immediately rub the cut garlic over the surface of the bread and drizzle with a little olive oil. Spoon some of the tomatoes on top of each slice, season with salt and pepper and top with some torn basil leaves. Serve immediately.

Other toppings for bruschette

Red and Golden Peppers with Basil ⓥ

You need 2 red and 2 golden peppers, halved, cored and seeded. Grill them over the barbecue as described on page 65, or under the grill indoors, until the skin loosens and begins to fleck with black. Strip off the papery charred skin first if you wish – I often leave it on – then with a sharp knife cut the peppers into ribbons. Season the peppers then put a mixture of colours on each bruschetta, drizzle over a little balsamic vinegar and olive oil and top with a piece of basil or rocket leaf.

Artichoke Paste and Black Olives ⓥ

Spread each bruschetta with a generous amount of Artichoke Paste, page 28, or use a good quality bought artichoke paste. Top with black olives.

Black and Green Olive Pâté ⓥ

Spread each bruschetta fairly generously with bought black or green olive pâté, or make Tapenade, page 33, with black or green olives (or some of each). Top with whole olives or leaves of flat-leaf parsley.

Sun-Dried Tomato and Feta Cheese

Good quality sun-dried tomato paste makes a good topping. Spread it lightly over each bruschetta and top with a little crumbled feta cheese.

Avocado with Rocket ⓥ

Halve an avocado then remove the stone and scoop out the flesh. Roughly mash the flesh with a squeeze of lemon juice and sea salt and pepper to taste. Alternatively, use Guacamole, page 32. Top each bruschetta with the avocado and a few rocket leaves dipped lightly in vinaigrette.

Grilled Aubergine Bruschette with Coriander Salsa Ⓥ

These aubergine slices are served on a piece of toasted ciabatta bread, topped with Coriander Salsa and served with Barbecue Sauce.

ingredients

2 medium–large aubergines, stalks cut off

salt

double quantity of Lemon and Olive Oil Marinade, page 20

Coriander Salsa, page 110

Barbecue Sauce, page 115

2 ciabatta loaves, halved lengthways

Cut the aubergines lengthways into slices about 6mm / ¼ inch thick. Sprinkle with salt, leave for about 1 hour to remove the air pockets, then rinse off the salt with cold water and pat the aubergine dry. Put into a shallow dish, cover with the marinade, and leave for 1 hour, turning once or twice to make sure the slices are well covered.

Make the salsa and barbecue sauce as described on pages 110 and 115.

TO BARBECUE OR GRILL:
Remove the aubergine from the marinade and cook on the barbecue until brown and crisp – about 4 minutes each side. Toast the ciabatta on the cut side until lightly browned – about 1 minute. Place a couple of aubergine slices and a few spoons of coriander salsa on top of each ciabatta then return to the grid to toast the base. Under the grill, cook the aubergine on both sides as above. Toast both sides of the ciabatta under the grill before topping with the aubergine and salsa. Serve with barbecue sauce alongside.

Goat's Cheese Toasted Sandwich

serves 4

Melting goat's cheese in crunchy bread: it's great eaten straight from the grill as a first course or an accompaniment to grilled Mediterranean vegetables.

ingredients

125g / 4oz firm goat's cheese log

8 slices of bread from a large loaf – a 'country'-style bread – I prefer white for this

olive oil

Mash the goat's cheese, including the rind, and spread over 4 of the slices of bread, keeping it at least 6mm / ¼ inch away from the edges. Cover with the remaining slices to make sandwiches and press down.

TO BARBECUE OR GRILL:
Brush the sandwiches on both sides with olive oil. Place them on the barbecue grid over hot coals or under a hot grill; when one side is brown and crisp – in a minute or two – turn the sandwiches over to brown the other side. Serve immediately, whole or quickly cut into 2 or 4 pieces.

Garlic Baguette

serves 4–6

Although this can be cooked on the barbecue, it's often more practical to save space by baking it in the oven where it can be kept hot. I've given both cooking methods – the choice is yours.

ingredients

125g / 4oz soft butter

3–4 garlic cloves

1 large baguette

Beat the butter with a wooden spoon until it's light and creamy, then crush the garlic and mix it in. Or put the whole peeled garlic cloves into a food processor with the butter and whiz to a cream. Slice the baguette at 2.5cm / 1 inch intervals without cutting right through the bottom. Pull back the pieces and spread the cut sides the garlic butter. Wrap the loaf in foil. The loaf can be prepared up to this point and kept for several hours before baking or grilling. It can also be frozen for 2–3 weeks – let it thaw out for several hours at room temperature before baking.

TO BAKE OR BARBECUE:
To cook in the oven, bake at 200°C / 400°F / gas 6 for 20–30 minutes, until the bread is hot and crisp on the outside.

To barbecue, place the foil parcel on the side of the barbecue where it's not too hot and cook for about 15–20 minutes, turning it to cook it all over, until the bread is piping hot, the butter melted and the crust crisp and charred in places.

Grilled Garlic Flat Breads

serves 4

Quick to make, these are a tempting starter to nibble while the rest of the food is cooking. Try them with one of the dips on pages 28–33.

ingredients

4 tablespoons olive oil

2 garlic cloves, crushed

1 tablespoon chopped fresh flat-leaf parsley

sea salt and freshly ground black pepper

4 flat sesame or white pitta breads

Mix together the olive oil, garlic, parsley and a little salt and pepper – this is the topping for the breads. Make cuts 1cm / ½ inch apart on the top of each pitta bread without cutting right through into the second layer.

TO BARBECUE OR BAKE:
Put the breads on the grid cut-side down and grill for 1–2 minutes. Flip the pittas over, spoon the olive oil mixture over the cut top and cook for a further 1–2 minutes until piping hot all through.

To cook them in the oven, spread the cut side with the olive oil mixture and simply bake for 5–10 minutes at 200°C / 400°F / gas 6.

Tomato and Cheese Pizza

makes 1 large pizza – for 2–4

This is one of my favourite dishes to make on the barbecue. It's surprisingly quick and easy to do and popular with everyone. The advance preparation – making the dough and the tomato sauce – is not nearly as difficult or time-consuming as you might think. Both freeze well, so if you get really organized, you could have some stashed away ready for next time.

ingredients

350g / 12oz strong unbleached white flour

7g / ¼oz sachet dried easy-blend yeast

2 teaspoons salt

½ teaspoon sugar

225ml / 8fl oz warm water

a little extra flour for kneading, as necessary

olive oil

FOR THE TOPPING:

Tomato Sauce, page 114

125g / 4oz grated Cheddar or mozzarella cheese

about 12 black olives

Combine the flour, yeast, salt and sugar, add the warm water and mix with your hands, a wooden spoon or in a food processor until a dough forms.

Knead the dough by hand for 5 minutes on a clean work-surface, flouring the work-surface as necessary to stop the dough sticking, or use the dough hook on the food processor.

Oil the surface of the dough lightly with your hands, place it in a deep bowl, stretch some clingfilm over the top and leave in a warm place until it has doubled in size: 1–2 hours, depending on the temperature.

Punch down the dough, knead for 1–2 minutes, then oil it lightly and put it back into the bowl as before. Leave it to rise again: this time it will take only about 45 minutes.

Prepare the tomato sauce and have it hot for when you make the pizza.

TO BARBECUE:

Knead the dough lightly and roll out thinly into a circle. I cook it straight on a fine-mesh grid (well-oiled) over the barbecue but you could use an oiled baking tray that fits on top of the grid. Cook the pizza until the underside is golden brown – about 10 minutes – then flip it over. (If you have a barbecue with a lid, you won't need to turn the pizza, although turning it does give a particularly crisp result.)

Spread the hot tomato sauce over the cooked top of the pizza and sprinkle with the grated cheese and olives. The pizza is done when the second side, underneath, is browned. The cheese will probably melt in the heat but won't get brown. Serve at once in thick wedges.

Other toppings for pizza

You can use all your favourite toppings but remember that they won't have time to cook on top of the pizza: you need to use ingredients that can be eaten raw or that have already been cooked. Sweetcorn, sliced canned artichoke hearts, sliced sun-dried tomato, roasted red or golden peppers, roasted mushrooms, cooked asparagus, cooked spinach, drained canned pineapple, and of course herbs such as oregano, thyme, basil, and finely sliced garlic – all make excellent toppings.

Variations

Garlic Pizza Bread

Mix 3 tablespoons olive oil with 2–3 crushed garlic cloves and set aside. Roll out the dough to a circle as described, cook the first side, then flip it over. Make long cuts on the surface about 1cm / ½ inch apart without going right through the dough and pour the oil and garlic mixture over the top. Cook until the underside is browned.

Calzones

Make the dough as described, divide it into 4 and roll out each piece to a circle about 20cm / 8 inches in diameter. Spread with Tomato Sauce (page 114), top with 3–4 tablespoons grated mozzarella or Cheddar cheese, then fold the dough over like a Cornish pasty. Brush lightly with oil. Place on the grid to cook one side, then flip it over and cook the other.

Nan Bread

Add 1 teaspoon cumin seeds and 1 teaspoon ground coriander to the flour when you make the dough. When it's ready, divide into 4 and roll out each piece into a tear-drop shape. Bake on an oiled baking sheet or, better I think, directly on a fine-mesh grid over the barbecue. When the underneath is browned, flip the nan breads over to cook the other side.

Cheese and Onion Pizza Bread

After the dough has risen for the second time, knead 50g / 2oz coarsely grated cheese and 2 tablespoons finely chopped onion into it. Roll it out and cook on the barbecue, flipping it over when the underside is done. If you like, sprinkle with sliced black olives and some sprigs of fresh thyme before serving. (Illustrated on page 31.)

Rosemary and Raisin Pizza Bread

After the dough has risen for the second time, knead 50g / 2oz raisins and 1 tablespoonful of chopped fresh rosemary into it. Roll it out and cook on the barbecue, flipping it over when the underside is cooked. Sprinkle with coarse sea salt and a little extra chopped fresh rosemary before serving. (Illustrated on page 31.)

Skewers and Kebabs

A skewer is convenient for keeping **small morsels of food** together as you cook them. Food on skewers also looks **colourful and attractive**, although you do need to put the skewers together with consideration for cooking times as well as for looks. **Cherry tomatoes**, for instance, which look pretty and are often used in barbecue photographs, are unsuitable in practice because they cook so much more quickly than anything else on the skewer, reducing to skin and watery mush in an instant. If you want to use them, they need to be on a skewer on their own, or with other **quick-cooking ingredients**.

It's fun to make up skewers with a variety of ingredients. As long as you choose foods that will cook in roughly the same amount of time, **you can't go wrong**. Or cut longer-cooking items, such as onions, more thinly than the faster-cooking ingredients. Occasionally, you need to **par-boil** a vegetable first – for example the Tandoori Potato Skewers, page 47 – but usually **trimming and slicing** is sufficient.

Fresh herbs between the vegetables on the skewers look pretty but soon burn during cooking. The only herbs that stand up to the heat are **bay**, **rosemary**, and perhaps **sage**, all of which are strongly flavoured and need to be used sparingly. I have used **woody sprigs of rosemary**, about 30 cm/ 12 inches long, stripped of their leaves except for the tips, as skewers. The result is wonderful for a special occasion, **both aromatic and eye-catching** – but you need a plentiful supply of rosemary from a mature bush.

I find it's best to **marinate** the ingredients (see pages 18–23) before putting them on the skewer. Metal or wooden skewers can be used; **soak wooden ones** in cold water for 30 minutes first to prevent them from burning – they can be washed afterwards and reused if you wish. **Metal skewers** have the advantage of conducting heat to the centre of the food, speeding up cooking time. Food can rotate vexingly as you turn the skewer: if you have enough, use **two skewers** for each kebab to keep the ingredients in place.

Garlic Mushroom Skewers

makes 8 skewers

This is a great way of jazzing up ordinary button mushrooms. They absorb a marinade well and become deliciously juicy and full of flavour. I particularly like them prepared with a garlic marinade but some of the others also work extremely well: try the Honey, Mustard and Balsamic Vinegar or the Balsamic Vinegar and Ginger marinades, page 23, for a darker and more intense flavour. Serve with hot bread as a first course or as a side dish.

ingredients

48 button mushrooms, washed and patted dry

Lemon and Garlic Marinade, page 20

Put the mushrooms in a shallow dish. Cover with the marinade, stirring to make sure they are all coated. Leave for at least 30 minutes. Thread 6 mushrooms on to each skewer, shaking off and keeping any excess marinade.

TO BARBECUE OR GRILL:
Cook the skewers on the barbecue or under a hot grill for about 10 minutes, until the mushrooms are cooked through and browned all over. Baste with marinade during the cooking time and spoon any remaining marinade over the mushrooms before serving.

Left to right: Wild Mushroom Skewers, Mixed Vegetable and Halloumi Skewers (page 44) and Asparagus and Oyster Mushroom Kebabs (page 47)

Wild Mushroom Skewers

makes 8 skewers

The mixed 'wild' mushrooms that you can sometimes buy at supermarkets can be used if the genuine article is unavailable. Serve with lots of bread. You can make this into a main course by serving with Wild Rice Salad, page 96, or Polenta, page 85, cooked until it is well charred, and crème fraîche and a juicy tomato and basil salad.

ingredients

48 assorted wild mushrooms, or 48 bite-sized pieces if mushrooms are large

Lemon and Pepper Marinade, page 20

Wash the mushrooms or mushroom pieces, pat dry and put in a shallow dish. Cover with the marinade, stirring to make sure they are all coated. Leave for at least 30 minutes. Thread 6 mushrooms or pieces of mushroom on to each skewer, shaking off and keeping any excess marinade.

TO BARBECUE OR GRILL:
Cook the skewers on the barbecue or under a hot grill for about 10 minutes, until the mushrooms are cooked through and browned all over. Baste with marinade during the cooking time and spoon any remaining marinade over the mushrooms before serving.

Mixed Vegetable and Halloumi Skewers

For a simple but delicious meal, serve two skewers per person with cooked rice, Garlicky Mashed Potatoes, page 66, or bread, and a cool salad; or allow one per person as a first course or side dish. (Illustrated on page 42.)

ingredients

450g / 1lb halloumi cheese

2 firm slender courgettes, cut into 1cm / ½ inch thick circles

125g / 4oz button mushrooms, washed and patted dry

Sara's Marinade, page 23

2 red peppers, seeded and cut into strips

fresh basil leaves, to serve

Cut the cheese into 16 cubes of about 2cm / ¾ inch. Do this carefully because halloumi breaks easily. Put the halloumi, courgettes and mushrooms into a shallow dish, cover with the marinade and stir gently to make sure all the pieces are coated. Cover and leave for at least 1 hour.

Thread the halloumi, courgettes, mushrooms and pepper slices on to the skewers. Shake any excess marinade back into the dish.

TO BARBECUE OR GRILL:
Put the skewers on the grid over hot coals or under a hot grill to cook for 7–10 minutes or until brown and charring on the edges, turning them during this time to cook evenly, and brushing with extra marinade as necessary to prevent the vegetables and cheese drying out. Pour any remaining marinade over the skewers before serving garnished with basil leaves.

Marinated Tofu Kebabs

makes 4 skewers

If you normally find tofu a little lacking in flavour, try this recipe: it makes tofu crisp and well flavoured. Serve these kebabs in warm pitta, or with cooked rice and Satay Sauce, page 112, or with Oriental Rice Noodle Salad, page 96.

ingredients

250g / 9oz packet of firm tofu

Honey, Mustard and Balsamic Vinegar Marinade, page 23

Cut the block of tofu into 16 cubes of about 2cm / ¾ inch. Do this carefully because tofu breaks easily. Put the tofu into a shallow dish, cover with the marinade and stir gently to make sure all the pieces are coated. Cover and leave for at least 1 hour, longer for a more pronounced flavour – I have successfully left it for 8 hours.

Thread the tofu on to the skewers, shaking any excess marinade back into the dish.

TO BARBECUE OR GRILL:
Put the skewers on the grid over hot coals or under a hot grill to cook for 7–10 minutes or until brown and charring on the edges, turning them during this time to cook evenly, and brushing with extra marinade as necessary to prevent the tofu drying out. Pour any remaining marinade over the tofu before serving.

Aubergine Kebabs (V)

makes 8 skewers

Cooked this way, aubergine has a tender sweetness and almost melts in your mouth. It's very good put straight from the skewers into hot pitta bread.

ingredients

2 medium–large aubergines

double quantity of Balsamic Vinegar and Ginger Marinade, page 23

4 tablespoons chopped fresh coriander

Slice off the stalks of the aubergines. Cut them in half lengthways, then cut each half into 12 chunky pieces, making 48 in all. Sprinkle with salt and leave for 1 hour to remove the air pockets. Rinse under cold water, pat dry and put into a shallow dish. Cover with the marinade, stirring gently to make sure all the pieces are well coated, and leave for 30 minutes to 2 hours.

Thread 6 aubergine chunks on to each skewer, shaking excess marinade back into the dish.

TO BARBECUE OR GRILL:
Put the skewers on the grid over hot coals or under a hot grill to cook for 7–10 minutes or until golden brown and charring on the edges, turning them during this time to cook evenly, and brushing with extra marinade as necessary to prevent the aubergines drying out. Pour any remaining marinade over the aubergines before serving garnished with fresh coriander.

Asparagus and Oyster Mushroom Kebabs

makes 8 skewers

These can be served on their own at the beginning of the meal, perhaps with some hot garlic bread; they also make a tasty accompaniment to other dishes such as Cashew Nut and Sun-Dried Tomato Burgers, page 76. Quick Hollandaise Sauce, page 117, also goes well with them. You need to use asparagus spears that are thick enough to get the skewer through – slim ones break easily. Because asparagus is tricky to thread, I find metal skewers better to use than wooden ones: they tend to be finer and sharper. (Illustrated on page 42.)

ingredients

350g / 12oz oyster mushrooms, washed and patted dry

8 thick spears of asparagus, each cut into 4 pieces

double quantity of Lemon and Olive Oil Marinade, page 20

Tear the mushrooms into 12 even-sized pieces and put into a shallow dish with the asparagus. Cover with the marinade, turning gently to make sure all the pieces are well covered, and leave for at least 30 minutes. Thread the mushrooms and asparagus alternately on to 8 (preferably metal) skewers, saving excess marinade.

TO BARBECUE OR GRILL:
Put the skewers on the grid over hot coals or under a hot grill to cook for 10–15 minutes or until to your taste, turning them during this time to cook evenly and brushing with extra marinade as necessary to prevent them drying out. Pour any remaining marinade over the skewers before serving.

Tandoori Potato Skewers

makes 4 skewers

These crisp potatoes with a spicy coating make an unusual accompaniment to burgers. Try them, too, with Nan Bread, page 39, Yogurt and Herb Sauce, page 107 and Mixed Tomato Salad, page 99.

ingredients

24 baby new potatoes, scrubbed

Tandoori Paste, page 24

This is one occasion where a vegetable needs to be par-boiled before grilling. Boil the potatoes until you can just get the point of a skewer or knife into them: about 5 minutes for very tiny potatoes, maybe 7–10 minutes for larger ones. Drain well and allow to cool.

Thread the potatoes on the skewers then coat them all over with the paste – fingers are best for this.

TO BARBECUE OR GRILL:
Cook on the grid over medium-hot coals for 15–20 minutes, until the potatoes are crisp and brown, turning the skewers during this time so that they cook evenly.

Vegetables

Most vegetables, from **early spring chicory** and **asparagus** to **late summer peppers** and **aubergines** and **autumnal mushrooms**, barbecue well. The flavour is enhanced by caramelization of the vegetable's natural sugars and extra tastes can be introduced with marinades.

Most vegetables can be barbecued or grilled raw, so preparation is easy: just wash the vegetables, trim them as little as possible, marinate them for 30 minutes or so, or simply brush with olive oil and a squeeze of lemon juice. A barbecue with a lid is helpful if you are grilling larger pieces or whole vegetables, ensuring that they cook right through to the centre without burning on the outside. However, whereas most meat needs to be thoroughly cooked, most vegetables (except **potatoes** and **aubergines**) can be eaten raw. So if they sometimes turn out to be a bit on the crunchy side, more like hot salads than tender cooked vegetables, they can still be enjoyed.

Vegetables make superb first courses – **asparagus**, for instance, marinated briefly with **lemon** then quickly seared and eaten while the **saffron risotto cakes** and **golden stuffed peppers** are cooking for the next instalment. Or you could serve the asparagus as an accompanying vegetable alongside **marinated halloumi cheese** for instance, perhaps with a **tomato salad** on the side. Or **asparagus** could become the star of the show, lots of it, as much as you can get on your grill, served with foaming hollandaise sauce and warm ciabatta bread: what could be nicer on an early summer day?

Think of artichokes, in the late summer, cooked on the grill so that you can bite right into them with no fiddly messing around with individual leaves; a mixed grill of summer vegetables; **red peppers stuffed with feta cheese and black olives; open-cap mushrooms with blue cheese filling** – to mention just a few. Add accompaniments such as **hot bread, creamy dips or sauces, refreshing salads or salsas,** and you get some idea of the many tempting meals that you can build around barbecued vegetables.

Because **vegetables are so versatile,** most of the dishes that follow could be served as starters, accompaniments or main courses, depending on what else you are serving with them. So I decided to present them simply in alphabetical order. Throughout the section I have given suggestions for what to serve them with, according to the role you want them to play in your meal.

Sicilian Artichoke Feast

serves 4

Spiky Sicilian artichokes have large hearts, so are best for this; if you can't get them, other types can be used, preferably the purplish 'black' artichoke. A sharp yogurt and wine sauce complements them perfectly; as does crème fraîche, a ripe blue Stilton or a salty pecorino. To eat these artichokes, you bite into them from the stalk end, eating as much of the delicious tender heart as you can, then discarding the leaves.

ingredients

6 spiky Sicilian artichokes on long stalks

225g / 8oz shallots, unpeeled, with root ends cut off

Spanish Red Wine Marinade, page 18

24 small garlic cloves, squashed flat with a fork

large bunch of fresh or dried oregano

large bunch of fresh or dried thyme

Pecorino Sauce, page 117, to serve

Handle the artichokes with care because 'spiky' certainly describes them: it's a good idea to trim the points off the outside leaves with scissors before you start. Cut the artichokes into quarters, slicing right down through the stalks, and cut out the spiky choke at the centre. (You can use the stalks to hold them by when eating.) Par-boil the artichoke quarters for 5–10 minutes to take off the rawness, then put into a shallow dish with the shallots, cover with the marinade and leave for 45–60 minutes.

Remove the artichokes and shallots from the marinade, shaking excess marinade back into the dish, and press one of the squashed garlic cloves into the centre of each artichoke quarter.

TO BARBECUE OR GRILL:

Put the artichokes cut-side down on a fine-mesh grid on a barbecue, nestle the shallots among them and place the thyme and oregano on top (they give off a wonderful scent). Cover the barbecue with its lid and cook for 5–10 minutes. Then lift off the herbs and turn the artichokes to cook the other cut-side. Brush each with a little more marinade, sprinkle with sea salt, replace the herbs and cook, again covered, for a further 5–10 minutes. If you're cooking them under a grill, place the herbs on the rack, place the artichokes on one cut-side on top and nestle the shallots among them. Turn the artichokes after 5–10 minutes on to the other cut-side, brushing with a little reserved marinade and sprinkling with sea salt.

About 5 minutes before the artichokes are ready, make the pecorino sauce as described on page 117 – quickly done on the cooker indoors – then serve the artichokes with the sauce spooned over them and the shallots alongside, to be slipped out of their skins.

Globe Artichokes with Tomato and Garlic Paste (V)

serves 4

A red wine marinade and a thick coating of tomato and garlic paste imparts an extra Mediterranean flavour to young globe artichokes. They make a wonderful first course, with hot grainy bread, or they can be served as a side dish alongside Risotto Cakes, page 80, or Herby Potato Cakes, page 79, with some salad and a little crème fraîche.

ingredients

4 globe artichokes

a Red Wine Marinade, page 18

large bunch of fresh or dried oregano

large bunch of fresh or dried thyme

Tomato and Garlic Paste, page 24

Quarter the artichokes, slicing right down through the stalks, and cut out the spiky choke at the centre. (You can use the stalks to hold them by when eating.) Par-boil the artichokes for 5–10 minutes to take off the rawness. Put them into a shallow dish, cover with the marinade and leave for 45 minutes. Make the paste as described on page 24.

TO BARBECUE OR GRILL:
Remove the artichokes from the marinade, shaking excess back into the dish. Place the artichokes, one cut-side towards the heat, on the barbecue or on a tray that fits under the grill. Cook for about 5–10 minutes then turn to cook the other cut-side. When the artichokes are almost done, remove from the heat and spread the cut surfaces with the tomato and garlic paste.

Place the thyme and oregano, for their scent, over the artichokes if you're cooking them on a barbecue or under them if you're cooking them under a grill. Grill for a further 5–10 minutes until the artichokes are completely tender, and the paste is hot.

Grilled Asparagus with Lemon and Pepper Marinade (V)

serves 4 as a starter, 2 as part of a main course

These make a wonderful starter or accompanying vegetable, or you can serve them as a main course with Quick Hollandaise Sauce or Pecorino Sauce, page 117, and bread, Wild Rice Salad, page 96, or Garlicky Mashed Potatoes, page 66. You will need a fine-mesh grid for the top of your barbecue to prevent the asparagus falling through the bars.

ingredients

450g / 1lb asparagus

Lemon and Pepper Marinade, page 20

Wash the asparagus and put into a shallow dish. Pour the marinade over, then use your fingers to turn the asparagus in the marinade so it gets coated all over. Cover and leave for 30–45 minutes.

TO BARBECUE OR GRILL:
Remove the asparagus from the marinade, shaking excess back into the dish. Put the asparagus on the barbecue or under the grill for about 10 minutes, or until just tender and slightly charred, turning as necessary. Serve the asparagus with the remaining marinade poured over it.

Grilled Asparagus with Baby Sweetcorn

serves 4

ingredients

450g / 1lb thin green asparagus

450g / 1lb baby sweetcorn

Lemon and Garlic Marinade, page 20

wedges of lemon to serve

Ordinarily I'm not fond of baby sweetcorn, but this recipe, where the baby sweetcorn are marinated with garlic, mixed with asparagus and grilled until brown and crisp, is far from ordinary; indeed, it's delectable. You need a fine-mesh grid to make this.

Put the asparagus and sweetcorn in a shallow dish, cover with the marinade and leave for 45 minutes.

TO BARBECUE OR GRILL:
Take the vegetables out of the marinade, shaking excess liquid from them. Spread the asparagus and sweetcorn out on the barbecue or under the grill and cook until just tender and charred in places, turning them as necessary: about 10 minutes. Serve at once, with wedges of lemon.

Thai Aubergine in Coconut Marinade

serves 4

Aubergine is one of the most successful vegetables to barbecue. The secret is to cut it fairly thinly, as described, so that it absorbs the flavours of a marinade well and cooks quickly, with lovely charred bits that add to the taste. Here it is in Thai mode, delectable with Oriental Rice Noodle Salad, page 96, and some hot Red Chilli Sauce, page 112; Thai Sweetcorn Fritters (page 78), too, if you have the time for them.

ingredients

2 medium aubergines

salt

Thai Coconut Marinade, page 22

chopped fresh coriander, to serve

Cut the aubergine into pieces about 6mm / ¼ inch thick and 2.5 x 5cm / 1 x 2 inches across. Put the pieces into a colander, sprinkle with a little salt and leave over a bowl for 30 minutes or so. Then rinse and pat dry. Put the aubergine into a shallow dish and cover with the Thai marinade; leave for 1 hour.

TO BARBECUE OR GRILL:
Remove the aubergine pieces from the marinade, shaking off and saving the excess. Put them on a fine-mesh grid over a barbecue or under a grill. You will probably have to cook the aubergine in batches, for 4–5 minutes on the first side until browned, then on the other side for roughly the same amount of time until tender. As the pieces are done, put them into a bowl with the rest of the marinade. Scatter with the coriander and serve.

Aubergine with Halloumi and Mint

serves 4 as a main course

The first time I made this I used mint because I hadn't any basil. The result was a pleasant surprise – all the flavours work together really well. Serve as a main course with bread and another grilled vegetable, such as Fire-Roasted Tomatoes (page 70), or a salad.

ingredients

2 medium aubergines

salt

double quantity of Balsamic Vinegar Marinade, page 23

450g / 1lb halloumi cheese

1 bunch of fresh mint, or 4 tablespoons chopped fresh mint

2–3 tablespoons olive oil

Slice the stalks off the aubergines and cut them into pieces about 6mm / ¼ inch thick and 2.5 x 5cm / 1 x 2 inches across. Put the pieces into a colander, sprinkle with a little salt and leave over a bowl for 30 minutes to remove the air pockets. Then rinse and pat dry. Put the aubergine into a shallow dish and cover with the marinade; leave for 1 hour.

Cut the cheese into slices a shade thicker than the aubergine. Roughly chop the mint if it is in a bunch.

TO BARBECUE OR GRILL:

Remove the aubergine pieces from the marinade, shaking the excess back into the dish. Put them on a fine-mesh grid over a barbecue or under a grill. Brush the cheese slices with olive oil and place them on the grid, keeping everything in a single layer. (If your grill isn't big enough, do the aubergine first, in two batches if necessary, then the halloumi.) Cook until browned on one side, then turn over and cook the other side. The aubergine and halloumi take roughly the same amount of time to cook: 5–10 minutes each side. When they're done, put them on a plate, pour the rest of the marinade over them and scatter with the mint.

Variation

Aubergine is also very good prepared like this but without the halloumi, then served with Goat's Cheese and Herb Dip, page 30 or, for vegans, creamy Hummus, page 32, White Bean Dip, page 30, or Guacamole, page 32.

Baby Aubergines Japanese Style (V)

serves 4

If baby aubergines are not available use larger ones cut into pieces about 6mm / ¼ inch thick and 2.5 x 5cm / 1 x 2 inches across. Serve with Marinated Tofu Kebabs, page 45, Oriental Rice Noodle Salad, page 96 and perhaps the Dipping Sauce on page 115 for a barbecue with a Japanese flavour.

ingredients

450g / 1lb baby aubergines

salt

Miso Marinade, page 19

2 tablespoons sesame seeds

1 teaspoon sea salt

Cut the aubergines in half, cutting through the stalks if you can. Sprinkle the cut surface with salt, leave for about 30 minutes to remove the air pockets then rinse and pat dry. Spread the aubergine halves with the marinade and leave for a further 30–60 minutes.

Meanwhile roast the sesame seeds and salt together in a small saucepan over a moderate heat, stirring for a minute or two until the seeds start to 'pop' and jump. Remove from the heat and crush with a pestle and mortar if you have one, otherwise with the back of a wooden spoon on a board. Keep on one side.

TO BARBECUE OR GRILL:
Cook the aubergines on a fine-mesh grid over a barbecue or under a grill, marinaded side up (whether the heat source is above or below – it works fine both ways), for 5–10 minutes. Sprinkle with the crushed sesame seeds and salt, and serve.

Baby Aubergines Japanese Style, Japanese Dipping Sauce (page 115) and Oriental Rice Noodle Salad (page 96)

Spicy Butternut Squash (V)

serves 4

Lovely spicy wedges of squash: eat as a starter; as a main course with Beautiful Bean Salad, page 92, and hot bread, or an accompaniment to Risotto Cakes, page 80.

ingredients

1 large or 2 small butternut squash

Tandoori Paste, page 24

Halve the squash, scoop out the seeds and slice into wedges like a melon. Coat the cut sides of the squash with the tandoori paste, and leave on one side for about 15 minutes or until you are ready to cook.

TO BARBECUE OR GRILL:
Cook the squash on the grid over medium-hot coals until lightly browned on each cut-side, turning as necessary: about 5 minutes altogether. Put the pieces of squash on the grid skin-side down and cook for a further 5–10 minutes, or until the flesh is cooked right through and tender. (Or cook in the same way under a grill.) Serve at once.

Warm Salad of Grilled Cauliflower, Watercress and Salty Pecorino

serves 4

ingredients

1 large cauliflower, very fresh, some outer leaves removed

Lemon and Garlic Marinade, page 20

125g / 4oz pecorino Romano cheese, grated

bunch of watercress, tough stalks removed

Vinaigrette, page 88

A main course salad, inspired by Castelvetro, the great seventeenth-century Italian cookery writer. Serve with hot bread – perhaps one of the garlic breads from page 37 or 39 made on the barbecue – and Mixed Tomato Salad, page 99.

Divide the whole cauliflower into florets then slice these into bite-sized pieces. Put in a shallow dish, cover with marinade and leave for 30 minutes, moving the pieces around once or twice.

TO BARBECUE OR GRILL:

Remove the cauliflower from its marinade and barbecue (use a fine-mesh grid if there's a danger of losing any pieces) or grill until *al dente* and beginning to brown; move the pieces around so that they cook evenly. Put the warm cauliflower into a bowl with the watercress, pecorino cheese and enough vinaigrette to moisten. Toss gently and serve immediately.

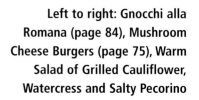

Left to right: Gnocchi alla Romana (page 84), Mushroom Cheese Burgers (page 75), Warm Salad of Grilled Cauliflower, Watercress and Salty Pecorino

Grilled Chicory and Fennel with Bay Leaves and Tomato Marinade ⓥ

serves 4

The chicory and fennel are marinated briefly in a simple tomato mixture, then spread with a piquant paste when partially cooked. Choose fresh white chicory, slim and pointed. This dish takes time to cook so you really need a barbecue with a lid, and it's most practical served as a main course with some cheese, a dip from pages 28–33, and some hot bread.

ingredients

4 fennel, halved

8 medium heads of chicory, halved

Tomato and Lemon Marinade, page 22

16 fresh bay leaves

bunch of fresh dill

Tomato and Garlic Paste, page 24

2–3 teaspoons dill seeds

Put the fennel and chicory in a shallow dish and cover with the marinade. Leave for 45 minutes.

Remove the vegetables from the marinade, shaking excess back into the dish to use later. Tuck a fresh bay leaf and a sprig of fresh dill between two of the outer leaves of each chicory half.

TO BARBECUE OR GRILL:

Place the chicory and fennel on a fine-mesh grid, cut-sides towards the heat, with the remaining fresh dill sprigs on top of them if you're using a barbecue or underneath them if you're grilling them. Cook over a moderate heat, with the barbecue lid on, for about 12 minutes, until the chicory and fennel are tender but not browned, brushing them with marinade as necessary to prevent them drying out.

Remove the vegetables from the grid, spread the paste over them and return them to the heat for a further 10–12 minutes, again with the lid on if over the barbecue, until cooked but still crisp. Serve any remaining marinade as a sauce and scatter the dish with dill seeds.

Stuffed Chillies

serves 2–4

Large, mild, green chillies, sometimes called anaheims, are delicious stuffed. You can also stuff other types of chilli but if the chillies are smaller than anaheims you will need more of them: 16–24 sanchos, for instance, as in the picture below and on page 63. The larger the chilli, the milder the taste; it might be advisable to test them first.

ingredients

8 anaheim chillies, or 16–24 smaller chillies such as sanchos

200g / 7oz feta cheese

16 black olives, stoned and chopped

4 tablespoons olive oil

8 sprigs of fresh oregano

Slit the chillies down one side and scoop out the white core and seeds, leaving the stalk intact. Cut the feta into small cubes and mash with the olives. Dip each chilli in olive oil, insert a sprig of oregano and stuff with the cheese and olive mixture.

TO BARBECUE OR GRILL:
Put the chillies on a grid over the coals or under a hot grill and cook for about 10 minutes until tender, the skin brown and blistering. Serve hot.

Variation

You can use strips of feta cheese without the olives, if preferred: cut the strips to fit the chillies. Or use one of the cheese or bean dips on page 30.

Courgettes in Yogurt and Mint Marinade with Crème Fraîche and Dill

serves 4

The yogurt marinade makes the courgettes melt in the mouth, and the remainder, mixed with crème fraîche and dill, makes a luscious sauce. Serve on a bed of hot couscous or brown rice or with hot sesame bread and a leafy salad; or try it with the Wild Rice Salad on page 96.

ingredients

8 large courgettes, cut into batons

Yogurt and Mint Marinade, page 22

4 tablespoons roughly chopped fresh mint

FOR THE SAUCE:

200g / 7oz carton of crème fraîche

juice of ½ lemon

4 generous sprigs of fresh dill, chopped

sea salt and freshly ground black pepper

Put the courgette batons in a shallow dish and cover with the marinade. Leave for at least 30 minutes, or for a really tenderizing effect up to 3 hours, moving the strips around gently from time to time.

TO BARBECUE OR GRILL:
Remove the courgettes from the marinade, shaking excess back into the dish. Place the courgettes on a fine-mesh grid over the barbecue or under a grill and cook on both sides until tender and browned: 5–7 minutes.

Meanwhile make the sauce by combining the remaining marinade with the crème fraîche, lemon juice and dill; season to taste. Sprinkle the courgettes with the chopped mint and serve with the sauce.

Grilled Fennel
with Goat's Cheese

serves 2–4

A dish as delicious as it is simple. Serve with dark rye bread.

ingredients

2 large fennel

Lemon and Pepper Marinade made with white wine, page 20

Goat's Cheese and Herb Dip, page 30, to serve

Cut the fennel in half and then cut down into pieces no more than 3mm / ⅛ inch thick. Place in a shallow dish and cover with marinade. Leave for 30–60 minutes.

TO BARBECUE OR GRILL:
Shake off and reserve excess marinade. Spread the fennel out in a single layer on a fine-mesh grid over the barbecue or under the grill, and cook on both sides until tender and slightly charred: about 5 minutes on each side. Transfer to a large dish and pour the remaining marinade on top. Serve with the dip alongside.

Variation

Fennel Marinated in Vermouth and Juniper

Use Vermouth and Juniper Marinade, page 19, instead of the Lemon and Pepper Marinade. Serve with Wild Rice Salad, page 96, and Soured Cream Dip, page 29.

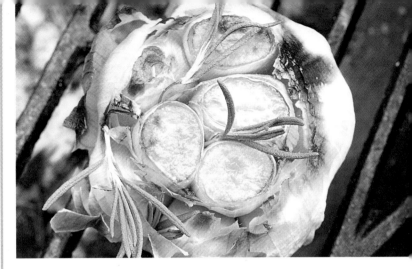

Whole Garlic
Grilled with Rosemary   (V)

serves 4

This gives you tender garlic pulp which you can easily squeeze out of its skin on to bread to eat as a starter or accompaniment to other grilled dishes.

ingredients

4 large garlic bulbs

1 tablespoon olive oil

4 sprigs of rosemary

Cut about 6mm / ¼ inch off the top of the garlic bulbs, exposing the tops of the cloves. Par-boil the whole bulbs for about 10 minutes, or until they are tender when pierced with a sharp knife or skewer. Drain well and brush the tops with the olive oil.

TO BARBECUE OR GRILL:
Grill the garlic on the barbecue, cut-side towards the heat, for 4–5 minutes until lightly browned. Then tuck a sprig of rosemary into each bulb and grill with the uncut side towards the heat for a further 3–5 minutes, until the bulb is browned underneath. To cook under a hot grill, brown the underside first, then the top, taking care not to burn the rosemary. Serve immediately, with plenty of bread.

Open Mushrooms with Red Pepper Pesto
serves 4

Open mushrooms provide a succulent base for a tasty topping: here I've used red pepper pesto, which is easy to make (see page 108), though you could buy it if you prefer. Serve with hot mixed-grain bread and salad or try it with Wild Rice Salad, page 96.

ingredients

12 large cup-shaped mushrooms, wiped, stems cut level with gills

Lemon and Garlic Marinade, page 20

Red Pepper Pesto, page 108

12 small basil leaves

Place the mushrooms in a shallow dish, pour over the marinade, moving the mushrooms to coat all over. Leave to marinate for at least 30 minutes.

TO BARBECUE OR GRILL:
Shake off – and reserve – any excess marinade from the mushrooms. Put the mushrooms over the barbecue cup-side (gill-side) down and cook them for 4–5 minutes, or until they are beginning to brown, then turn them over so that they are cup-side up. Put a spoonful of pesto into each mushroom and cook for a further 3–4 minutes or until tender right through. If you are using the grill, again cook the mushrooms cup-side down first, then turn cup-side up and spoon in the pesto. The heat is coming from a different direction but it won't make any difference to the end result. Garnish each with a basil leaf and serve at once.

Variations

Grilled Open Mushrooms with Gorgonzola

Use Gorgonzola Dip, page 28, instead of the Red Pepper Pesto.

Grilled Open Mushrooms with Goat's Cheese

Use the Goat's Cheese and Herb Dip, page 30, instead of the Red Pepper Pesto.

Grilled Open Mushrooms with Butter Bean and Black Olive Dip (V)

Replace the Red Pepper Pesto with Butter Bean and Black Olive Dip, page 30. Garnish each mushroom cup with a black olive.

Grilled Open Mushroom 'Pizzas'

Grill the mushrooms as described then put a spoonful of Tomato Sauce, page 114, into each instead of the Red Pepper Pesto, covering all the black gills. Sprinkle with grated cheese of your choice and top with black olives.

Open Mushrooms with Red Pepper Pesto, and Stuffed Chillies (page 60)

Grilled Fresh Porcini Mushrooms

(V)

serves 4

Porcini are not cheap to buy but make a memorable late summer treat. This recipe comes from Marcella Hazan, who says: 'No fresh mushroom, and no wild mushroom, morels and chanterelles included, remotely approaches the bosky flavour and satin texture of porcini. And no cooking method liberates so much of that flavour as grilling or sautéing with olive oil and garlic. Whether on the grill or in the sauté pan, porcini must cook slowly until tender throughout. High heat stuns the flavour and withers the texture. Good olive oil is indispensable. In the recipe you will find chestnut leaves listed as an optional ingredient. The leaves must be from the Spanish (or sweet) chestnut tree (Castanea sativa), not the common chestnut tree.'

ingredients

900g / 2lb fresh porcini mushrooms

12 tablespoons olive oil

4 teaspoons finely chopped garlic

2 tablespoons chopped fresh parsley

sea salt and freshly ground black pepper

**10–12 chestnut leaves, optional
(if available)**

Pare away from the mushroom stems any part that has soil attached. Wash the mushrooms rapidly under running water and pat thoroughly dry with kitchen paper. Detach the stems from the caps and cut the stems lengthways into slices about 1cm / ½ inch thick.

TO BARBECUE OR GRILL:

Turn on the grill, if cooking indoors, or light the charcoal. The coals will be ready for cooking when they have become evenly coated with white ash. You need a medium rather than a flaming heat.

Put the mushroom caps, with their round side up, and the stems in a single layer on a grilling rack and place the rack about 20cm / 8 inches away from the source of heat. After 5–7 minutes, turn the caps and stems over and cook for 4–5 minutes more. Move them around the rack as necessary to ensure even cooking.

If you are grilling over coals, season the mushrooms now with most of the olive oil, and the garlic and parsley, salt and grindings of pepper, and cook for 1–2 more minutes, depending on the thickness of the caps and the heat of the coals. About half a minute before removing the mushrooms from the fire, moisten the chestnut leaves (if you have them) with olive oil and place them over the mushrooms. Serve the mushrooms on top of the leaves.

If you are using a grill pan indoors, remove the rack from the pan. Place the chestnut leaves, if used, on the bottom of the pan, brushing them lightly with olive oil. Transfer the hot mushrooms from the rack to the leaves (or the bottom of the pan if you have no leaves) with the round side down. Pour the remaining olive oil over the mushrooms, then sprinkle with the garlic and parsley, salt and generous grindings of pepper. Return to the grill for another minute or two, then serve on top of the leaves.

Grilled Peppers with Thyme

serves 2–4

Peppers are one of the easiest vegetables to cook on the grill or barbecue. They make a colourful accompaniment to other grilled foods, and can be also be served simply with slivers of Parmesan, a leafy salad and hot ciabatta.

ingredients

2 red peppers

2 golden peppers

1 bunch of fresh or dried thyme

olive oil

1 garlic clove, crushed

2 tablespoons balsamic vinegar or freshly squeezed lemon juice

salt and freshly ground black pepper

Halve and seed the peppers, then cut into quarters or eighths. Press a good sprig of thyme into each and brush with olive oil.

TO BARBECUE OR GRILL:
Lay the peppers on the grid over the coals or under a grill, with the skin side nearest the heat source. Cook for about 10–15 minutes, until the skin is charred in places and blistering, and the flesh tender. Remove them from the grill and place in a bowl with the garlic, vinegar or lemon juice and some salt and freshly ground black pepper. Serve hot, warm or at air temperature.

Red Peppers Stuffed with Feta Cheese and Black Olives

serves 4

This is also good made with firm goat's cheese instead of feta. Either way, it's excellent with Garlic Potato Wedges, page 66, Risotto Cakes, page 80 and perhaps Tabbouleh, page 93. (Illustrated on page 98.)

ingredients

4 red peppers

FOR THE FILLING:

450g / 1lb feta cheese, diced

175g / 6oz kalamata olives, stones removed to make about 125g / 4oz

juice of ½ lemon

2 tablespoons olive oil

1 garlic clove, crushed

1 tablespoon dried oregano

Cut the peppers in half through the stalks, then remove the seeds, leaving the stalks intact. Mix all the filling ingredients together and set aside.

TO BARBECUE OR GRILL:
To barbecue the peppers, stuff them with the feta mixture, place them on the grid over the coals, rounded side towards the heat, and cook until the skin is charred in places and the filling is hot: about 10 minutes. To cook under a grill, first grill the peppers, rounded side towards the heat, until the skin is charred. Then turn the peppers over, fill them and grill them until the feta is golden brown and the peppers completely cooked: about 10 minutes. Serve immediately.

Garlicky Mashed Potatoes with Olive Oil (V)

serves 4–6

These garlicky potatoes supply an element both tangy and creamy that complements many barbecued dishes. If you like mashed potatoes I recommend a potato ricer, a gadget like a large garlic press through which you put the cooked potatoes a few at a time. Quick and easy – and you'll never have lumpy potatoes again. It's also invaluable for preparing the Herby Potato Cakes on page 79, one of the most popular recipes in this book.

ingredients

900g / 2lb potatoes

3–4 garlic cloves and a little salt

4 tablespoons olive oil

salt and freshly ground black pepper

Peel the potatoes and cut into even-sized pieces. In a saucepan, cover the potatoes with water and boil until very tender. Meanwhile, crush the garlic with the flat blade of a knife and work it into a paste with a little salt. Drain the potatoes, keeping the liquid. Mash the potatoes until smooth – a potato ricer is excellent for this – then add the crushed garlic, half the olive oil and enough of the reserved cooking water to make a creamy consistency. Check the seasoning, adding salt and pepper as necessary. Turn the mixture into a shallow serving dish and pour the remaining olive oil over the top.

Variation

Garlicky Mashed Potatoes with Thyme (V)

Add 1–2 tablespoons chopped fresh or dried thyme to taste to the mashed potatoes with the salt and pepper.

Garlic Potato Wedges (V)

serves 4

Although you can bake potatoes on the barbecue – see variation below – I find this method, of cooking them in wedges, more satisfactory: they cook more quickly and become golden and crisp. They are excellent on their own, with sea salt, a leafy salad and mayonnaise or a creamy dip, or as an accompaniment to other dishes.

ingredients

900g / 2lb potatoes, scrubbed

Lemon and Garlic Marinade, page 20

crunchy sea salt

Cut the potatoes lengthways in half, then cut each half lengthways into thirds or quarters to make wedge shapes. Put the potatoes into a shallow dish, cover with the marinade and leave for 30 minutes.

TO BARBECUE OR GRILL:
Shake off and save any excess marinade, and place the potato wedges on the barbecue or under the grill. Cook until golden brown and tender, turning as necessary: this will take 25–30 minutes. Put into a serving dish, sprinkle with crunchy sea salt and serve immediately.

Variation

Baked Potatoes

Medium-sized potatoes (about 125g / 4oz each) will bake on the grid in about 1 hour – it helps if the barbecue has a lid. They cook quicker on a metal skewer: the metal conducts heat through the centre of the potato.

Alternatively, par-bake the potatoes in the oven indoors for about 45 minutes then finish them off on the barbecue, letting them get nicely brown and crisp. Serve split open with one of the savoury butters on page 25.

Chunky Chips of Sweet Potatoes with Chilli-Lime Marinade

(V)

serves 4

Tender sweet potato wedges with a hot and tangy marinade. Good on their own as a first course or as an accompaniment to other vegetables or burgers. A chicory salad, hot bread and blue cheese go well with them, too.

ingredients

900g / 2lb sweet potatoes, scrubbed

Chilli-Lime Marinade, page 20

fresh coriander and lime wedges, to garnish

Cut the sweet potatoes lengthways in half then down into sixths or eighths to make 3-sided wedge-shaped chips. Put the chips into a shallow dish, cover with the marinade and leave for 30 minutes.

TO BARBECUE OR GRILL:
Shake off and save any excess marinade, and place the chips on the barbecue or under the grill. Cook until golden brown and tender, turning as necessary: this will take 25–30 minutes. Transfer to a serving dish, pour any remaining marinade over and garnish with the coriander and lime wedges.

Radicchio alla Griglia (V)

serves 4

In this classic recipe I've substituted lemon, garlic and sun-dried tomato paste for the anchovies. Serve as a first course with flakes of Parmesan cheese and hot bread or with Polenta, page 85, or one of the Risotto Cakes on page 80.

ingredients

Tomato and Garlic Paste, page 24

4 tablespoons walnut oil

juice of ½ lemon

1 radicchio, quartered

25g / 1oz walnuts

Mix the tomato paste with the walnut oil and lemon juice. Spread the paste over the radicchio, covering it thoroughly. Leave for 30 minutes while the flavours develop. Meanwhile, toast the walnuts under a grill and crush roughly.

TO BARBECUE OR GRILL:
Cook the radicchio, cut-side towards the heat, for about 2 minutes, until slightly wilting; turn to grill the other side for 1 minute. Transfer to a plate, scatter with the grilled walnuts and serve.

Radicchio with Raspberry Vinegar Marinade (V)

serves 4

A piquant dish using raspberry vinegar that contains whole raspberries; if you can't get this, use ordinary raspberry vinegar and add fresh or frozen berries.

ingredients

1 radicchio, quartered

Raspberry Vinegar Marinade, page 23, whole raspberries kept to one side

Put the quarters of radicchio in a dish and cover with the marinade; leave for about 30 minutes.

TO BARBECUE OR GRILL:
Remove the radicchio from the marinade, shaking excess back into the dish. Put the radicchio on a grill pan or barbecue, cut-side towards the heat. Cook for about 2 minutes, until it begins to wilt. If you are cooking over the barbecue, turn the radicchio over so that it is cut-side up, spoon any remaining marinade and the reserved raspberries over the radicchio and cook for 1 more minute. If cooking under the grill, there's no need to turn the radicchio – it's already cut-side up – before spooning the marinade and raspberries over. Serve at once.

Grilled Sea Kale in White Wine with Porcini and Tarragon Mustard Marinade

Ⓥ

serves 4

I wanted to experiment with sea kale for this book, although at first sight it seemed unappealing. However, its appearance is misleading – the resulting dish was exquisite. If sea kale is not available it can be substituted with white and purple asparagus. Serve with Polenta, page 85, brushed with olive oil and barbecued. You need a fine-mesh grid for this and preferably a barbecue with a cover.

ingredients

4 tablespoons olive oil

7 tablespoons medium-dry white *vin de pays*

4 garlic cloves, crushed

40–50g / 1½–2oz dried porcini mushrooms

3 bunches of sea kale

White Wine and Tarragon Mustard Marinade, page 19

1 tablespoon tarragon mustard

1 bunch of tarragon

First attend to the porcini: warm 2 tablespoons of the olive oil with the white wine and garlic, immerse the porcini and leave to steep, off the heat, for 20 minutes.

Put the sea kale in a dish, cover with the marinade and leave for 30 minutes.

TO BARBECUE OR GRILL:

Remove the sea kale from the marinade and coat with the tablespoonful of tarragon mustard. Arrange a bed of tarragon on a fine-mesh grid and put the sea kale mixture on top. Drain the porcini mushrooms, keeping the liquid, and place on top of the sea kale. Grill for about 20 minutes, until cooked through. Serve with any remaining marinade and porcini soaking liquid poured over.

Three Ways with Sweetcorn ⓥ

serves 6

Sweetcorn is a favourite at barbecues. Choose the freshest corn – shiny, juicy cobs with no dryness. Allow ½ or a whole cob per person, depending on what else you are having with it – it makes a good first course or can be included in a mixed vegetable grill such as the one on the facing page.

TO COOK DIRECTLY ON THE GRID:

Peel off the green leaves and silky threads. Leave the sweetcorn whole or cut it into halves or circles. Brush with oil or a marinade and put on the grid. It will brown in places, caramelizing, tasting sweet and smoky. Serve with olive oil, melted butter or one of the marinades such as lemon pepper to spoon over. If you like, cut each cob into two or three pieces and thread on to skewers (metal ones conduct the heat better) before grilling as above. On skewers it cooks quicker and is easier to hold.

TO COOK IN FOIL:

Peel off the green leaves and silky threads and brush the sweetcorn with oil or rub with butter. Season and wrap completely in foil. Cook on the grid for 15–20 minutes, until tender, turning the packages from time to time to ensure even cooking.

TO COOK IN ITS OWN LEAVES:

For a sweet, tender, more delicate result, use the leaves of the sweetcorn as a natural wrapper. Cook on the grid for about 15 minutes, until tender.

Fire-Roasted Tomatoes ⓥ

serves 4

These make a colourful and juicy accompaniment to other grilled foods. The secret is not to overcook them – they need to heat through without collapsing. Use large, firm tomatoes, but not beefsteak ones.

ingredients

4 large tomatoes

1–2 tablespoons olive oil

1–2 teaspoons dried thyme

salt and freshly ground black pepper

Halve the tomatoes through the middle, brush the cut sides lightly with olive oil, sprinkle with dried thyme and salt and grind some pepper coarsely over the top.

TO BARBECUE OR GRILL:

Place the tomatoes cut-side up on the barbecue grid or under a grill; cook for 4–5 minutes, or until they are heated through and the flesh is just beginning to part from the skin. If you have a fine mesh grid on your barbecue, cook them cut-side down. Serve immediately.

Mixed Vegetable Grill

serves 4

A feast of vegetables … and plenty of different ways to serve them. Try them just as they are, with hot bread; or with one of the substantial salads such as Creamy Potato Salad, page 103, Wild Rice Salad, page 96, a bean or lentil salad, pages 92 and 103, or Tabbouleh, page 93. Alternatively, serve them with a creamy dip such as Butter Bean and Black Olive, or Goat's Cheese and Herb, page 30; or Crème Fraîche and Spring Onion Sauce, page 107; or shave some Parmesan over the top. Halloumi cheese, page 82, is lovely with this grill, too. You need a large grill, with a fine-mesh grid on it, to accommodate all the vegetables. And of course, you can vary the mixture of vegetables any way you choose.

ingredients

1 aubergine, cut into pieces of 2.5 x 5cm / 1 x 2 inches and about 6mm / ¼ inch thick

salt

2 large courgettes, cut lengthways into quarters or eighths

2 red peppers, seeded and cut into quarters or eighths

1 fennel, trimmed, quartered, then each quarter cut into thin sections

2 red onions, cut into 6mm / ¼ inch rounds

8 flat mushrooms, washed and patted dry

4 tomatoes, halved

double quantity of Lemon and Garlic Marinade, page 20

3–4 tablespoons chopped fresh parsley or torn basil

Put the aubergine into a colander, sprinkle with a little salt and leave over a bowl for 30 minutes to remove the air pockets. Then rinse and pat dry. Put the aubergine and all the other vegetables into one or more shallow dishes and cover with the marinade; move the vegetables around so that they are coated all over. Leave for 1 hour.

TO BARBECUE OR GRILL:
Drain the vegetables, saving the marinade. Cook the vegetables in batches, turning them over when they are browned on one side, and transferring them to a serving dish when they are cooked. Pour the reserved marinade over them. When they are all cooked, sprinkle with the chopped herbs and serve.

Burgers, Sausages and Savoury Cakes

In this section you will find recipes for **vegetarian burgers, sausages** and **savoury cakes** which **taste superb** and are enhanced by the **charring effect** of the grill and barbecue. Also included are **halloumi cheese** and **polenta** which, while not 'burgers', fill that role very well in the **vegetarian barbecue**.

The burgers have been created to hold together well on the barbecue but, being **light and moist**, they are not indestructible and they respond best to **a gentle touch**. They can be made **thick**, for serving with grilled vegetables, fresh salads and cooling or spicy sauces; or fairly **flat and thin**, for serving in a bun, with all the usual trimmings. **Children, in particular, love them**, especially the Chilli Bean Burgers, page 74 (though some may prefer them made without the chilli), Herby Potato Cakes, page 79, or Risotto Cakes, page 80, sandwiched in a **warm sesame seed bun** with mayonnaise, tomato ketchup, slices of tomato and lettuce. Glamorgan Sausages (page 79), Polenta (page 85) and Gnocchi alla Romana (page 84) all go down very well with the younger generation, too.

Whichever burgers, sausages or savoury cakes you choose, and whether you make them thick or thin, brush them lightly all over with olive oil before grilling or char-grilling and handle them gently.

Burgers, sausages and polenta all freeze satisfactorily but tend to become crumbly afterwards and so need extra care in cooking. Before freezing them I shape them and coat them with crumbs (if required), then place them in a single layer on a plate or baking sheet and leave them, uncovered, in the freezer until firm. Then I store them in a rigid polythene box in the freezer for up to four weeks. They can be used straight from the freezer or slightly thawed; just make sure you grill or barbecue them for long enough to cook the inside. If undercooked, they won't hurt you, but they won't be nearly as nice as when **delectably crisp** on the outside, **piping hot** and tender within.

Chilli Bean Burgers

makes 6

(v)

This recipe, specially created for the barbecue, is based on well-cooked short-grain brown rice whizzed in a food processor with other ingredients to make a mixture that holds together. It's important both to cook the rice and to process the mixture thoroughly. The crumb coating also helps hold the burgers together. The basic recipe can be adapted to make a variety of different burgers: see below.

ingredients

75g / 3oz short-grain brown rice

1 onion, finely chopped

1 tablespoon olive oil

1 garlic clove, crushed

425g / 15oz can red kidney beans, drained

1 tablespoon sun-dried tomato paste

¼ teaspoon chilli powder, or to taste

sea salt and freshly ground black pepper

a few soft breadcrumbs to thicken the mixture, if necessary

3–4 tablespoons dried breadcrumbs for coating

olive oil for brushing

Wash the rice then put it into a saucepan with 200ml / 7fl oz water. Bring to the boil, then cover, turn the heat down as low as possible and leave to cook undisturbed for 45 minutes. The rice will be tender and all the water absorbed.

Fry the onion in the oil for 10 minutes until soft but not browned. Add the garlic and cook for a minute or two longer. Then remove from the heat and put into a food processor with the beans, rice, sun-dried tomato paste, and chilli powder, salt and pepper to taste. Process the mixture until it holds together firmly. If it's a little on the wet side you can add a few breadcrumbs, but this probably won't be necessary. The mixture needs to be firm without being stodgy.

Divide the mixture into 6 portions and form each into a burger shape. Dip into dried crumbs, coating all over. Keep in a cool place until you are ready to cook.

TO BARBECUE OR GRILL:
Brush the burgers on both sides with olive oil and place on the grid over the coals or under a hot grill. Grill until they are crisp and brown, turning them over carefully with a fish slice to cook the second side.

Variations

Chickpea Burgers

Use a can of chickpeas instead of the red kidney beans and omit the sun-dried tomato paste and the chilli powder. Put a teaspoon each of ground coriander and ground cumin into the pan with the garlic; and add 2 heaped tablespoons chopped fresh parsley to the mixture when you process it.

Butter Bean and Black Olive Burgers

(v)

Replace the red kidney beans with butter beans, and the sun-dried tomato paste with 2 tablespoons black olive pâté. Omit the chilli powder.

Mushroom Cheese Burgers

ingredients

2 tablespoons olive oil

350g / 12oz button mushrooms, washed, patted dry and sliced

3 garlic cloves, crushed

225g / 8oz grated Cheddar cheese

2 eggs, beaten

salt and freshly ground black pepper

olive oil for grilling

FOR PREPARING THE TIN:

15g / ½oz melted butter

1 tablespoon dry grated Parmesan cheese

makes 4 x 10cm / 4in or 8 x 5cm / 2in burgers

These are moist and tasty. Be sure to cook the mushrooms for long enough, until all the moisture has gone. Use muffin or Yorkshire-pudding tins to pre-bake these burgers.

Preheat the oven to 180°C / 350°F / gas 4. Brush the 4 large compartments of a Yorkshire-pudding tin or the 8 smaller ones of a muffin tin with melted butter. Sprinkle with Parmesan cheese.
   Heat the olive oil in a saucepan, add the mushrooms and fry until tender and free from liquid: this may take 15 minutes or so. Add the garlic, cook for a minute or two longer, then remove from the heat. Stir in the cheese, egg and seasoning to taste. Divide between the tins, smoothing the surface of each cake. Bake for 10–15 minutes, until firm to the touch and lightly browned. Cool in the tins, then turn out.

TO BARBECUE OR GRILL:
Brush the burgers on both sides with olive oil. Place on the grid of the barbecue or under the grill and cook until browned, then turn over to cook the other side, brushing with a little more oil if necessary.

Goat's Cheese Burgers

makes 8

ingredients

225g / 8oz fresh white bread, torn into rough chunks

225g / 8oz firm goat's cheese log

4 tablespoons water

sea salt and freshly ground black pepper

olive oil for brushing

On its own, goat's cheese melts too much to cook on the barbecue. However, if you mix it with breadcrumbs you can form it into a burger which grills to perfection – crunchy and golden on the outside, moist and full of flavour within. Spoon a sweet sauce or marinade over the burgers after cooking: try Apricot and Lemon Sauce, page 112, or Sara's Marinade, page 23.

Put the bread and goat's cheese (including the rind) into a food processor and whiz until finely chopped. Add the water and whiz again to form a dough. Taste, season with salt and pepper and whiz again to incorporate the seasoning. Divide the mixture into 8 portions and shape into flat burgers. Keep cool until required.

TO BARBECUE OR GRILL:
Brush the burgers with olive oil. Cook them on a grid over the hot coals or under a hot grill, turning them with tongs until they are browned all over.

Walnut and Rosemary Burgers

(V)

makes 8

This holds together very well on the grid. People may joke about nut burgers but anyone who has eaten a good one knows it can be delicious. I love these with Radicchio alla Griglia, page 68 – re-creating a classic Tuscan combination of ingredients – along with Hollandaise Sauce, page 117, good bread and a herby green salad.

ingredients

175g / 6oz short-grain brown rice

1 onion, finely chopped

1 tablespoon olive oil

1 garlic clove, crushed

200g / 7oz walnuts

1 tablespoon chopped fresh rosemary

2 tablespoons soy sauce

sea salt and freshly ground black pepper

a few soft breadcrumbs to thicken the mixture, if necessary

5–6 tablespoons dried breadcrumbs for coating

olive oil for brushing

Wash the rice then put it into a saucepan with 400ml / 14fl oz water. Bring to the boil, then cover, turn the heat down as low as possible and leave to cook undisturbed for 45 minutes. The rice will be tender and all the water absorbed.

Fry the onion in the oil for 10 minutes until soft but not browned. Add the garlic and cook for a minute or two longer.

While the onion is cooking, put the walnuts under a hot grill for a minute or two until they are toasted.

Put the rice into a food processor with the onions and garlic, the walnuts, rosemary, soy sauce and some sea salt and pepper to taste. Process the mixture until it holds together firmly. If it's a little on the wet side you can add a few breadcrumbs, but this probably won't be necessary. The mixture needs to be firm without being stodgy.

Divide into 8 portions and form each into a burger shape. Dip into dried crumbs, coating all over. Keep in a cool place until you are ready to cook.

TO BARBECUE OR GRILL:
Brush the burgers on both sides with olive oil and place on the grid over the coals or under a hot grill. Grill until they are crisp and brown, turning them over carefully with a fish slice to cook the second side.

Variations

Cashew Nut and Sun-Dried Tomato Burgers

Replace the walnuts with cashew nuts and the fresh rosemary with 1 tablespoon dried basil. Omit the soy sauce. Add 1–2 tablespoons sun-dried tomato paste (according to taste) to the mixture in the processor.

Peanut Burgers

(V)

Use 200g / 7oz crunchy peanut butter instead of the walnuts and 4 heaped tablespoons chopped fresh parsley instead of the fresh rosemary. Omit the soy sauce.

Walnut and Rosemary Burgers, Frisée Salad with Croûtons (page 89) and Quick Hollandaise Sauce (page 117)

Thai Sweetcorn Fritters

(V)

makes 8

Try these with Thai Aubergine in Coconut Marinade, page 52, and Red Chilli Sauce, page 112.

ingredients

175g / 6oz short-grain brown rice

4 tablespoons chopped fresh coriander

2 lemongrass stalks – discard any tough outer layers and chop the rest

1 green chilli, seeded and chopped

sea salt and freshly ground black pepper

400g / 14oz can sweetcorn, drained

2 tablespoons coconut milk powder

a few soft breadcrumbs to thicken the mixture, if necessary

5–6 tablespoons dried breadcrumbs for coating

olive oil for brushing

Wash the rice then put it into a saucepan with 400ml / 14fl oz water. Bring to the boil, then cover, turn the heat down as low as possible and leave to cook undisturbed for 45 minutes. The rice will be tender and all the water absorbed.

Put the rice, coriander, lemongrass and chilli into a food processor with some salt and pepper to taste and whiz until the mixture holds together firmly. Transfer to a bowl and stir in the sweetcorn and coconut milk powder. If it's a little on the wet side, add a few breadcrumbs, though this probably won't be necessary. You need to end up with a firm mixture.

Divide into 8 portions, form each into a burger shape and dip in dried crumbs, coating all over. Keep in a cool place until you are ready to cook.

TO BARBECUE OR GRILL:
Brush the cakes on both sides with olive oil and place on the grid over the coals or under a hot grill. Grill until they are crisp and brown, turning them over carefully with a fish slice to cook the second side.

Herby Potato Cakes ⓥ

makes 8

These are popular with vegetarians and meat-eaters alike. It's a very simple mixture but there are two keys to success. First, it helps if you have a ricer – like a huge garlic press which you push the cooked potatoes through – because it results in very dry mashed potatoes which hold together well. A potato masher, however, will do (though never a food processor, which makes them gluey) – just make sure the potatoes are very dry and well mashed. Secondly, do use the full amount of fresh herbs. Try to include some tarragon, chervil, flat-leaf parsley and dill.

ingredients

900g / 2lb potatoes, peeled and cut into even-sized pieces

2 tablespoons chopped fresh herbs: tarragon, parsley, chervil and dill, for example

salt and freshly ground black pepper

5–6 tablespoons dried breadcrumbs for coating

olive oil for brushing

Cook the potatoes in water to cover until tender: about 15 minutes. Drain the potatoes them pass them through a ricer into a bowl or mash them. Add the chopped herbs and season to taste. Divide into 8 portions, form into flat cakes and coat well with dried breadcrumbs.

TO BARBECUE OR FRY:
Brush the cakes on both sides with olive oil, place on the grid over hot coals and cook until golden brown, turning them over to cook both sides: about 10–15 minutes in total. The cakes can be cooked under a grill but they are perhaps better fried if they are not to be barbecued.

Glamorgan Sausages

makes 8

These traditional cheese sausages hold together and cook beautifully on the barbecue. Make sure they are well brushed with oil before barbecuing to prevent sticking.

ingredients

150g / 5oz fresh white bread, torn into rough chunks

125g / 4oz Cheddar cheese, grated

1 medium onion, quartered

2 tablespoons chopped fresh flat-leaf parsley

1 heaped teaspoon Dijon mustard

2 tablespoons water

sea salt and freshly ground black pepper

olive oil for brushing

Put all the ingredients except the salt, pepper and olive oil into a food processor and whiz until they are finely chopped and form a dough. Taste, season with salt and pepper and whiz again to incorporate the seasoning. Divide the mixture into 8 portions and roll into sausages. Keep cool until required.

TO BARBECUE OR FRY:
Brush the sausages with olive oil. Cook them on the grid over the hot coals, turning them with tongs until browned all over: about 10 minutes all together. They are also good fried.

Risotto Cakes
makes 6

A risotto, well-flavoured and cooled, can be formed into 'cakes' that will cook on the barbecue, under the grill or in a griddle or frying pan without either falling apart or absorbing a great deal of oil. Combinations of flavourings and ingredients make possible numerous variations on the basic theme – some of my favourites follow.

ingredients

40g / 1½oz butter

1 onion, finely chopped

1 litre / 1¾ pints vegetable stock

325g / 11oz risotto rice

150ml / 5fl oz white wine

2 garlic cloves, crushed

50g / 2oz freshly grated Parmesan cheese, optional

2 tablespoons each of chopped fresh flat-leaf parsley, marjoram and tarragon

sea salt and freshly ground black pepper

olive oil for brushing

Melt the butter in a large saucepan, put in the onion, cover and cook gently, stirring from time to time, until the onion is tender and translucent but not browned: about 10 minutes. Meanwhile, pour the vegetable stock into another saucepan and bring to just below simmering.

Add the rice to the onions in the pan and stir over the heat for 1–2 minutes, then pour in the wine and stir until it is absorbed. Then pour in a ladleful of the hot vegetable stock and again stir until it is absorbed. Continue like this until you have used all the stock, adding it little by little: the whole process takes about 25 minutes.

Stir in the garlic, Parmesan cheese if you are using it, herbs and salt and pepper to taste. Remove from the heat and leave until cold. Check the seasoning, then divide the mixture into 6 portions and form each into a chunky croquette, like a fat sausage, pressing together well so that it holds its shape.

TO BARBECUE OR GRILL:
Brush the cakes on both sides with olive oil and place on the grid over the coals or under a hot grill. Cook until they are crisp and brown, turning them over carefully with a fish slice to do the second side. They can also be fried.

Variations

Wild Mushroom Risotto Cakes

Soak 15g / ½oz dried mushrooms in 150ml / 5fl oz boiling water for 20 minutes then drain, reserving the soaking water, and chop. The soaking water can be used as part of the vegetable stock: strain it through muslin or a kitchen-paper-lined sieve in case of grit. Add the mushrooms to the pan with the rice and continue as described. Omit the tarragon and marjoram and use parsley alone.

Saffron Risotto Cakes

Crush a good pinch of saffron strands, cover with a tablespoonful of boiling water and leave to steep while you cook the risotto. Add with the garlic and herbs.

Saffron Risotto Cakes, and Radicchio alla Griglia (page 68)

Grilled Halloumi Cheese

serves 4

Halloumi cheese does not melt when heated, so it's perfect for grilling and cooking on the barbecue. You can cut and skewer it but I prefer it cooked flat on the grid, like a burger: this way it gets delectably browned and charred. It's inclined to dry out, so needs to be brushed with oil or, better still, if you have time, to be soaked in a marinade for 30 minutes or so before cooking. Delicious with grilled vegetables and wedges of lemon or a tangy salsa, page 110.

ingredients

2 x 250g / 8oz packets of halloumi cheese

Lemon and Pepper Marinade, page 20, or olive oil for brushing

Drain the liquid in which the halloumi is packed and blot the cheese with kitchen paper or a clean cloth. Cut into slices approximately 6mm / ¼ inch thick – you will get about 8 from each packet. Put the slices into a shallow dish, cover with the marinade and leave for about 30 minutes; or simply brush the pieces lightly on both sides with olive oil just before cooking.

TO BARBECUE OR GRILL:
Drain off and reserve the excess marinade (if used). Lay the pieces of cheese on the grid over the barbecue or under a grill and cook until browned on one side, then turn over to do the other side. It takes 3–4 minutes to cook each side – the cheese is nicest when well browned and crisp. Serve with any remaining marinade poured over.

Variation

Grilled Halloumi with Rosemary

Cut the cheese into thicker pieces – each one about 1cm / ½ inch thick, so that you get 4 from one packet. Marinate or brush with oil as described, then stick a generous sprig of rosemary in the top of each piece. Grill as described, browning the bottom and sides of each piece.

Ricotta and Parmesan Slices

serves 4

Mild in flavour and fairly smooth in texture, these go with most grilled vegetables: try them with grilled asparagus and tomatoes for an early summer barbecue or, later in the season, with grilled peppers and thyme.

ingredients

250g / 8oz ricotta cheese

125g / 4oz freshly grated Parmesan cheese

1 egg

salt and freshly ground black pepper

olive oil for grilling

FOR PREPARING THE TIN:

15g / ½oz melted butter

1 tablespoon dry grated Parmesan cheese

Preheat the oven to 180°C / 350°F / gas 4. Line a 20cm / 8 inch square tin with non-stick paper, brush with melted butter and sprinkle with the dry grated Parmesan.

Mix together the ricotta, Parmesan and egg, and season with salt and pepper. Pour into the tin and smooth the surface. Bake for about 40 minutes, until firm to the touch and lightly browned. Cool in the tin, then turn out, strip off the paper and cut into squares or triangles.

TO BARBECUE OR GRILL:
Brush the pieces on both sides with olive oil. Place on the grid over hot coals or under a preheated grill and cook until browned on one side, then turn over to cook the other side, brushing with a little more oil if necessary.

Gnocchi alla Romana

serves 4–6

Or cheese fritters, as we know and love them in my family. They work very well over the barbecue. Make sure you flavour them well, and if possible use a non-stick saucepan for making the mixture – it makes washing up a lot easier. Good with Fire-Roasted Tomatoes, page 70, and Apricot and Lemon Sauce, page 112, or cooling Yogurt and Herb Sauce, page 107, plus a green salad.

ingredients

568ml / 1 pint milk

1 bay leaf

1 onion

150g / 5oz semolina

150g / 5oz freshly grated Cheddar or Parmesan cheese, or a mixture of both

2 teaspoons Dijon mustard

2 tablespoons chopped fresh flat-leaf parsley

sea salt and freshly ground black pepper

5–6 tablespoons dried breadcrumbs for coating

olive oil for brushing

Put the milk into a saucepan with the bay leaf and onion. Bring to the boil, then remove from the heat, cover and leave to infuse for 15–30 minutes. With a slotted spoon remove the bay leaf and onion, which you won't need any more, and return the pan to the heat. Bring to the boil, then sprinkle the semolina on top, stirring all the time with a wooden spoon. Let the mixture boil for about 4 minutes, stirring all the time, until it is so thick that the spoon will stand up in the middle. Remove from the heat and stir in the grated cheese, mustard and parsley. Season with salt and pepper.

Turn the mixture out on to a piece of non-stick paper and spread to a thickness of approximately 1cm / ½in. Leave in a cool place – or the refrigerator – for several hours until completely cold and firm.

Cut the mixture into shapes – triangles, fingers or circles, whatever you fancy. Dip them in the breadcrumbs, coating each piece well.

TO BARBECUE OR GRILL:
Brush the gnocchi with olive oil. Cook on the grid over hot coals or under a hot grill for about 5 minutes on each side, until crisp and brown.

Polenta

serves 4

When polenta, a grain, is cooked and allowed to set, it can be grilled like a burger and so take on the burger 'role' in a vegetarian barbecue. Polenta grain can be bought in two forms: ground to varying degrees of coarseness, or partially cooked, called 'instant' or 'quick'. The only difference is that the 'instant' ones, as you might expect, take less time to cook. You can also buy polenta that has been completely cooked and set into a fat golden sausage or slab. This can be a useful shortcut, especially served with gutsy, robust ingredients. But cooking your own is easy and has the advantage of allowing you to be adventurous with the flavourings: see the suggestions on the right.

Polenta is good grilled or barbecued then spread with black or green olive pâté, Tapenade, page 33, red or green Pesto, page 108, or Artichoke Paste, page 28. I like it cooked so that it's crusty and brown then served with a refreshing salsa, page 110, or something creamy such as crème fraîche or a garlicky mayonnaise. A Canadian favourite, which doesn't sound good until you try it and realize that it's magic, is barbecued polenta with maple syrup, served as a pudding.

Put the polenta into a heavy-based saucepan with the water and a little salt and mix to a smooth paste. Put the pan on the heat and bring to the boil, stirring. Then turn the heat down, partially cover the pan with a lid to prevent the mixture from spluttering everywhere, and leave to cook gently: 30 minutes, or 5 minutes if it's quick-cooking polenta – see the packet.

Turn the polenta out on to a lightly oiled baking sheet or piece of non-stick paper and spread and press to a thickness of about 1cm / ½ inch. Or pour the mixture into a lightly oiled 500g / 1lb loaf tin and smooth the surface. Leave in a cool place – or the refrigerator – for several hours or until completely cold and firm: the polenta in the tin will take longer.

Cut the flat polenta into shapes, or turn out the polenta from the tin and slice as required. Put the polenta into a shallow dish, cover with the marinade and leave for about 30 minutes; or simply brush the pieces lightly on both sides with olive oil just before cooking.

TO BARBECUE OR GRILL:
If the polenta is marinated, shake off any excess marinade. Cook on the grid over the coals or under a grill until browned, turning them to cook both sides.

ingredients

175g / 6oz polenta

575ml / 1 pint water

sea salt

Lemon and Pepper Marinade, page 20, or olive oil for brushing

Variations

Herb Polenta

Stir 2–3 tablespoons chopped fresh herbs into the polenta when you take it off the heat. Robust herbs such as thyme, rosemary, marjoram and oregano, along with some parsley, work best.

Olive Polenta

Add about 125g / 4oz chopped olives to the polenta when you take it off the heat. Both green and black olives are good. For best flavour, it's worth buying loose olives at the deli or a Middle-Eastern or Mediterranean store, and stoning them yourself.

Parmesan Polenta

Mix 125–175g / 4–6oz freshly grated Parmesan into the polenta when you take it off the heat. Try it with grilled asparagus, tomato salad and mayonnaise.

Salads

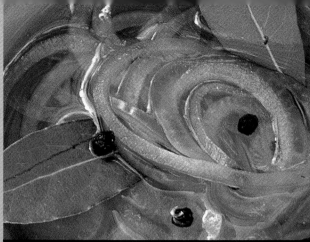

Salads provide a **welcome accompaniment to grilled food** and have the advantage that they can be largely or wholly prepared beforehand. They can, of course, be made from a wide range of ingredients, and in this section you will find both **light, refreshing salads** and **more substantial ones** made from **grains, noodles, beans, lentils** and **potatoes** – appetites increase in the **fresh air!**

Some salads, such as **coleslaw and tomato salad, can be dressed beforehand and are the better for it;** others, particularly those containing delicate leaves, need to be **tossed in the dressing at the last minute**. You can make up a quantity of dressing and add it to the salad as required – this is convenient when catering for large numbers. For smaller gatherings, I often mix **olive oil, lemon juice, balsamic or rice vinegar, garlic** and **seasoning** in a salad bowl then cross the **salad servers** on top and add the salad. This keeps the **delicate leaves** away from the dressing, while making it **easy to toss** and finish the salad just before eating it.

As time goes by I find my taste for dressings becomes lighter and lighter. Whereas I used to use three or four parts olive oil to one of vinegar, I now often use a half-and-half mixture of olive oil and vinegar, or vinegar plus lemon juice. This works if you use a light vinegar such as my favourite, **rice vinegar**, which is now quite easy to find thanks to the popularity of Eastern food. If the resulting dressing is too vinegary, the addition of **freshly squeezed lemon or lime juice** or even plain cold water usually makes it just right. A **light dressing** such as this goes particularly well with the **rich taste** of grilled and barbecued food, as does, even more simply, plain **balsamic vinegar**, as good a quality as you can afford. With balsamic vinegar, you really do get what you pay for.

Vinaigrette

makes about 300ml / ½ pint

It's often easiest to make a dressing straight into the salad bowl, but none the less it can be useful to have some vinaigrette already made up, either for dressing a salad quickly at the last minute or for serving separately in a jug. This dressing is lighter than some; the sweet balsamic vinegar and lemon juice or rice vinegar balance the olive oil. Proportions of oil and vinegar, and flavourings, are variable, to taste. It will keep for up to 2 weeks in the refrigerator.

ingredients

125ml / 4fl oz olive oil

125ml / 4fl oz balsamic vinegar

4 tablespoons freshly squeezed lemon juice or rice vinegar

1 garlic clove, crushed

sea salt and freshly ground black pepper

Put all the ingredients into a screw-top jar, put the lid on firmly and shake to combine.

Variation

Light Mustardy Vinaigrette

Add 2 tablespoons Dijon mustard to the mixture; it's best to start with this in a bowl and gradually stir in the rest of the ingredients to make a thick dressing.

Frisée Salad with Croûtons

serves 4

(V)

Here frisée lettuce is in a mustardy vinaigrette with the crunch of croûtons. Prepare the individual constituents ahead of time ready to put together at the last minute. A variation is to include a few leaves of radicchio with the frisée. Other variations are given below.

ingredients

1 or 2 heads of frisée

FOR THE CROUTONS:

light olive oil

4 slices of white or brown bread, crusts removed

MUSTARD VINAIGRETTE:

1 tablespoon best quality Dijon mustard

1–2 garlic cloves, crushed to a paste with salt

3 tablespoons red wine vinegar

6 tablespoons olive oil

freshly squeezed lemon juice, optional

sea salt and freshly ground black pepper

Wash the frisée, separating the leaves, shake dry and refrigerate to crisp until required.

Make the croûtons: cover the base of a frying pan with light olive oil and fry the slices of bread until golden brown and crisp on both sides. Drain and blot on kitchen paper to remove excess oil, and cut into 6mm / ¼ inch dice. Cool, then wrap in foil until required.

Make the dressing: put the mustard and garlic into a bowl, stir in the vinegar, then whisk in the oil a little at a time to make a smooth emulsion. Thin, if required, with a little freshly squeezed lemon juice (or water) and season with salt and pepper.

To finish the salad, tear the frisée into a salad bowl, spoon over enough dressing to moisten, toss gently, and add the croutons.

Variations

Rocket, Watercress or Basil Salad

(V)

Make as described, using rocket, watercress or basil instead of the frisée and omitting the croûtons.

Marinated Red Onion Rings (V)

serves 4–6

Red or purple onions blanched in boiling water then covered with vinegar turn bright pink – a vibrant accompaniment to grilled food. They will keep, covered, for a week or so in the refrigerator. This recipe comes from The Greens Recipe Book *by Deborah Madison.*

ingredients

3 small or 2 medium red onions, about 450g / 1lb

a kettleful of boiling water

6 tablespoons rice or white wine vinegar

6 tablespoons water

10 black peppercorns

2–3 bay leaves

Peel the onions, slice them into paper-thin rounds and separate the rings. Put the rings into a colander and pour the boiling water over them. Then rinse them under cold water and put into a bowl with the rice vinegar, water, peppercorns and bay leaves. Cover and refrigerate for at least 1 hour before serving.

Palm Heart Salad (V)

serves 4

I love canned palm hearts: I find their silky texture and slight sharpness (from the canning liquid) a beguiling companion to barbecued dishes. They need the simplest of preparation.

ingredients

400g / 14oz can palm hearts, drained

2–3 tablespoons Greek olive oil

juice of ½ lemon

sea salt and coarsely ground black pepper

1 tablespoon roughly chopped fresh flat-leaf parsley

Slice the palm hearts and put them into a bowl. Add the olive oil and lemon juice, sprinkle with a touch of sea salt and (more) coarsely ground black pepper. Leave in a cool place, then serve with a scattering of chopped parsley.

Salad of Cucumber, Mustard Seeds and Dill

(V)

serves 4

ingredients

2 cucumbers

1 medium-sized white onion

salt

1 tablespoon white mustard seeds

3 tablespoons vinegar: rice or white wine, preferably

1–2 teaspoons caster sugar

sea salt and coarsely ground black pepper

3–4 good sprigs of fresh dill, chopped

A perennial favourite of mine because of its clean taste and the absence of oil. You might describe it as a cross between a salad and a pickle; it combines the advantages of both.

Peel the cucumbers and onion and slice each into paper-thin rounds. Put the slices into a colander, sprinkle with salt and leave for 30–60 minutes to draw out excess liquid.

Press the cucumber and onion to squeeze out as much liquid as possible then put into a bowl with the mustard seeds, vinegar and caster sugar to your taste. Cover and leave for 1–2 hours – or overnight, if convenient. Just before serving, season and add the dill.

Beautiful Bean Salad

(V)

serves 4

ingredients

2 tablespoons olive oil

2 tablespoons balsamic vinegar

2 tablespoons tomato ketchup

2 teaspoons brown sugar

2 garlic cloves, crushed

salt and freshly ground black pepper

1 small purple onion, finely chopped

425g / 15oz can red kidney beans, drained and rinsed

425g / 15oz can cannellini beans, drained and rinsed

2 tablespoons chopped fresh flat-leaf parsley

The secret ingredient that makes this extra delicious is, believe it or not, tomato ketchup. It seems to make all the difference to the flavour, and you can defy your guests to guess what it is. Different varieties of bean can be used; I love mealy-textured red kidney beans as a base, as here, with another, contrasting bean.

Put the olive oil, balsamic vinegar, tomato ketchup, sugar and garlic into a bowl with some salt and pepper and mix together to make a dressing. Add the onion and the beans and mix gently to get the beans well coated with the dressing. Sprinkle with chopped parsley before serving.

Tabbouleh

(V)

serves 4–6

A salad of bulgur wheat, plumped in water, with plenty of chopped fresh parsley and mint, flavoured with lemon juice and olive oil. Proportions of wheat to herbs can vary, but the more parsley the better the salad. Other ingredients can be added: chopped tomato, diced cucumber (salted first as described in the Salad of Cucumber, Mustard Seeds and Dill, facing page), black olives, crushed garlic, sliced avocado, raw red or green pepper, purple onion – there are as many versions of this salad as there are cooks. Tabbouleh can be made well in advance – indeed, is all the better for it.

ingredients

225g / 8oz fine bulgur wheat

large bunch of flat-leaf parsley

8–10 sprigs of mint

2–3 spring onions

4 tablespoons olive oil

juice of 1 lemon

sea salt and freshly ground black pepper

Put the bulgur wheat in a bowl and cover generously with boiling water. Leave to soak and plump up for 20–30 minutes while you prepare the other ingredients.

Remove the stalks from the parsley and chop the leaves finely. Do the same with the mint. Trim and finely chop the spring onions.

Drain the plumped-up wheat thoroughly and pat dry with kitchen paper. Put the wheat into a bowl and add the parsley, mint, spring onion, olive oil and lemon juice. Mix thoroughly and season with salt and pepper. Cover and keep cool until needed.

Greek Salad

serves 4

ingredients

1 cucumber, peeled and diced

1 medium-sized white onion, finely sliced

450g / 1lb tomatoes, chopped

juice of ½ lemon

2–3 tablespoons Greek olive oil

50–125g / 2–4oz black kalamata olives

sea salt and coarsely ground black pepper

225g / 8oz feta cheese, diced

2–3 teaspoons dried oregano

Try this with hot garlic bread or home-made nan bread straight off the barbecue. The combination of hot bread with moist, salty feta cheese, cool cucumber and tomatoes is superb.

Put the cucumber, onion and tomatoes in a bowl and add the lemon juice, olive oil, black olives and salt and pepper to taste. Keep cool until needed. Just before serving, add the feta and sprinkle with dried oregano.

Middle-Eastern Vegetable Salad

(V)

serves 4

ingredients

bunch of spring onions, lightly trimmed

bunch of radishes, washed, leaves still attached

4 carrots, scrubbed, cut into batons

½ cucumber, cut into batons

sprigs of flat-leaf parsley

4 tomatoes, quartered

125g / 4oz chillies preserved in brine, drained

lemon wedges

Garden-fresh vegetables served with the minimum of preparation … Preserved chillies in brine make a tangy addition: buy them loose at a Middle-Eastern shop or deli. Serve the salad very cold.

Arrange the vegetables on a platter and garnish with lemon wedges.

Oriental Radish Salad

(V)

serves 2–4

This makes quite a small quantity, to be served more as a relish than a salad; for a larger quantity, simply double all the ingredients.

ingredients

2 bunches of radishes

4 tablespoons rice vinegar

bunch of spring onions, trimmed and chopped

2 tablespoons sesame seeds and 1 teaspoon sea salt, optional

Trim the radishes then slice thinly. Bring a saucepan of water to the boil, put in the radishes, bring back to the boil and simmer for 1 minute. Drain into a sieve or colander and immediately rinse under the cold tap to cool quickly. Shake excess water off the radishes and put into a bowl with the rice vinegar and chopped spring onions. If using the sesame seeds, roast them very briefly in a hot dry pan then crush with the sea salt – a pestle and mortar is best, or use the back of a wooden spoon on a board. Sprinkle over the salad just before serving.

Thai Sweetcorn Fritters (page 78), Red Chilli Sauce (page 112) and Oriental Radish Salad

Wild Rice Salad

serves 4–6

This goes very well with grilled vegetables. I particularly like it with grilled mushrooms and peppers – indeed, with any of the Mediterranean vegetable dishes in this book.

ingredients

50g / 2oz wild rice

175g / 6oz basmati rice

3–4 tablespoons chopped fresh flat-leaf parsley

FOR THE DRESSING:

2 garlic cloves, crushed

2 teaspoons honey

1 teaspoon soy sauce

1 tablespoon balsamic vinegar

1 tablespoon olive oil

salt and freshly ground black pepper

Cook the wild rice and the basmati rice in separate saucepans in plenty of boiling water. The basmati rice needs 8–10 minutes until it is tender, and the wild rice 35–40 minutes. In each case, drain the rice in a sieve, rinse under the cold tap and drain again. Put both rices in a bowl together.

While the rice is cooking you can make the dressing by combining all the ingredients with salt and pepper to taste. Pour the dressing over the rice, add the parsley and mix gently with a fork. Check the seasoning, and serve warm or at room temperature.

Oriental Rice Noodle Salad Ⓥ

serves 4

Light and refreshing, this makes an excellent accompaniment to any of the grills with an oriental flavour – Thai Sweetcorn Fritters, page 78, Aubergine Kebabs or Marinated Tofu Kebabs, page 45, for instance. (Illustrated page 54.)

ingredients

125g / 4oz transparent rice noodles

1 preserved red chilli – the kind you buy in a jar

4 spring onions, trimmed and very finely sliced

1 tablespoon toasted sesame oil

grated rind and juice of 1 lime

4 tablespoons roughly chopped fresh coriander

salt and freshly ground black pepper

Cover the noodles with boiling water, leave for 5 minutes to soak, then drain and rinse under the cold tap. Drain again, then put the noodles into a bowl. Remove the stem and seeds from the chilli and slice it finely. Add it to the noodles in the bowl along with the spring onions, sesame oil, lime rind and juice, coriander and salt and pepper to taste. Serve at once.

Spiced Rice Salad with Nuts and Seeds

serves 4

Basmati rice is here cooked gently by the absorption method and takes on the flavours of the spices and the golden colour of the turmeric.

ingredients

2 tablespoons olive oil

1 small onion, chopped

½ cinnamon stick

1 teaspoon cumin seeds

1 bay leaf

3 cardamom pods, lightly crushed

1 teaspoon turmeric

salt

200g / 7oz basmati rice

3 tablespoons roughly chopped fresh coriander, optional

FOR THE NUTS AND SEEDS:

25g / 1oz butter

100g / 3½oz flaked almonds

25g / 1oz pine nuts

25g / 1oz shelled pistachio nuts

15g / ½oz poppy seeds

15g / ½oz sunflower seeds

Heat the oil in a large, heavy-based saucepan, then put in the onion, cover and cook gently for 3–4 minutes, until the onion is beginning to soften but has not browned.

Bring 400ml / 14fl oz water to the boil.

Add the cinnamon stick, cumin seeds, bay leaf, cardamom pods, turmeric and half a teaspoon of salt to the onion in the saucepan. Stir over the heat for a few seconds, then add the rice and stir again over the heat. Pour in the boiling water – it will bubble vigorously – then cover, turn the heat down to very low and leave to cook gently for 10 minutes, until the rice is tender and the water absorbed.

Meanwhile, prepare the nuts and seeds. Melt the butter in a saucepan, put in the almonds and pine nuts and fry gently, stirring frequently, for about 4 minutes, until golden. Add the pistachio nuts and poppy and sunflower seeds, stir to cover in melted butter and remove from the heat.

Stir the rice with a fork. Just before serving, stir in the nuts, seeds and, if using, the coriander.

Kohlrabi Salad   (V)

serves 4

The crisp, juicy texture and clean flavour of kohlrabi, which looks like a vegetable from outer space, makes a welcome accompaniment to gutsy grilled dishes. The dressing contains no oil.

ingredients

2–3 kohlrabi

juice of 1 lemon

sea salt and coarsely ground black pepper

watercress or flat-leaf parsley, to serve, optional

Peel the kohlrabi as near the surface as possible, then cut into paper-thin rounds. Slice the rounds in half, like half moons. Put them into a bowl with the lemon juice and sea salt and coarsely ground pepper to taste. Chill until required. Serve the salad as it is, or with a border of watercress or flat-leaf parsley.

Mixed Tomato Salad   (V)

serves 4

Tomatoes of different types, ripeness, size and colour give variation of taste and texture to this simple salad.

ingredients

900g / 2lb mixed tomatoes: include red and yellow cherry tomatoes and one or two other types, some under-ripe

sea salt and coarsely ground black pepper

2–3 tablespoons Greek olive oil

juice of ½ lemon

8 basil leaves

Slice the tomatoes and put them into a bowl. Sprinkle with sea salt and coarsely ground black pepper, and the olive oil and lemon juice. Leave in a cool place for at least 30 minutes. Check the seasoning, tear the basil leaves over and serve.

Easy Crunchy Coleslaw

serves 4–6

ingredients

350g / 12oz white cabbage, shredded or coarsely grated

125g / 4oz carrots, grated

1 onion, finely sliced, optional

4 tablespoons mayonnaise or a mixture of mayonnaise and plain yogurt

a little freshly squeezed lemon juice, optional

salt and freshly ground black pepper

A classic accompaniment for burgers, the creamy freshness of coleslaw makes it a natural partner for charred vegetables, too. It's easy to make and the home-made version is so much nicer than the shop-bought.

Combine the cabbage, carrots and, if using, the onion, in a bowl. Stir in the mayonnaise or mayonnaise and yogurt to make a creamy mixture, adding a dash of lemon juice to moisten a little more if necessary. Season with salt and pepper. Serve at once or keep for up to 2 days in the refrigerator.

Red Peppers Stuffed with Feta Cheese and Black Olives (page 65) and Kohlrabi Salad

Salad of Chicory, Fresh Dill, Wild Rocket and Avocado (V)

serves 4

This salad needs plenty of dill and rocket, both used as vegetables rather than herbs, so buy them by the bunch if you can. Wild rocket has smaller leaves and a more delicate taste than the regular type, but the regular will do if you can't get the wild. It's a delectable salad, in any case: a perfect accompaniment to many grilled dishes.

ingredients

3 chicory

6–8 good sprigs of fresh dill, roughly chopped

bunch of rocket, wild if possible

1 or 2 garlic cloves

salt

1 large or 2 small ripe avocados

juice of ½ lemon

4 tablespoons Greek olive oil

sea salt and freshly ground black pepper

dash of balsamic vinegar, optional

Wash the chicory, separating the leaves. Wash the dill and rocket. Shake the leaves and herbs dry and put into a bowl. Crush the garlic to a paste with a little salt, add to the leaves and toss. Leave covered and cool until you want to serve the salad.

Just before serving, halve the avocado(s), remove the stone and skin and slice the flesh. Add to the bowl along with the lemon juice, olive oil, sea salt and pepper, and the balsamic vinegar for a touch of sweetness if you think the salad needs it.

Carrot Salad with Nuts, Raisins and Fresh Herbs (V)

serves 4

ingredients

450g / 1lb grated carrots

juice of 1 large orange or 6–8 tablespoons apple juice

2 tablespoons chopped fresh herbs – dill, parsley, tarragon, chervil, chives, lovage or mint for instance

50g / 2oz raisins or sultanas, optional

50g / 2oz pine nuts, toasted under the grill then cooled, optional

Grated carrots in fruit juice make a simple, fresh salad that's good with barbecued burgers. This salad can be varied to suit taste and occasion – the dried fruit and nuts, for example, make it more substantial.

Mix the grated carrots with the fruit juice and fresh herbs, along with the raisins or sultanas if using. Just before serving, add pine nuts, if you wish.

Salad of Chicory, Fresh Dill, Wild Rocket and Avocado

Peperonata

serves 4

Peperonata, that Italian stew a little like ratatouille but without aubergine and courgette, is delicious hot or cold. I also use it as a stuffing for peppers cooked on the barbecue: see the variation below.

ingredients

3 tablespoons olive oil

1 large onion, chopped

4 large red peppers

4 large golden peppers

2 garlic cloves, finely sliced

2 x 400g / 14oz cans tomatoes

sea salt and coarsely ground black pepper

dash of balsamic vinegar

1–2 tablespoons coarsely chopped flat-leaf parsley

Warm the oil in a large saucepan, put in the chopped onion, stir, cover and leave to cook gently for 10 minutes, until tender but not browned.

Meanwhile, halve the peppers and remove the stems, cores and seeds. Cut into 6mm / ¼ inch dice. Add to the tender onions along with the garlic. Stir, cover and cook for a further 10 minutes.

Pour the tomatoes into the pan and bring to a simmer, then leave to cook gently, uncovered, for 1–1½ hours, or until the consistency is quite thick and purée-like. (Cover the pan during this time and reduce the heat further if the mixture seems to be getting thick too quickly.)

Cool, then chill it if you want to serve it really cold. Taste and season with salt, pepper and a dash of balsamic vinegar. Serve scattered with the parsley.

Variations

Peperonata with Fennel

Use only 3 red and 3 golden peppers. Take 1 or 2 large fennel, pare the outside of tough, stringy parts and trim off the stem ends. Chop the fennel into small dice and add to the pan with the peppers.

Peperonata with Black Olives

Toss a handful of black olives into basic peperonata or peperonata with fennel before serving.

Golden Peppers Stuffed with Peperonata

Prepare the peppers for stuffing as described in the recipe for Red Peppers Stuffed with Feta Cheese and Black Olives on page 65. Stuff with peperonata instead and barbecue or grill in the same way.

Creamy Potato Salad

serves 4

Cool and creamy, this is great with grilled foods.

ingredients

700g / 1½lb potatoes, new or waxy, scrubbed but not peeled

1 tablespoon wine vinegar

3 tablespoons olive oil

salt and freshly ground black pepper

2 tablespoons mayonnaise

2 tablespoons yogurt, soured cream or crème fraîche

1–2 tablespoons chopped fresh chives

Cut the potatoes if necessary so that they are of even size. Cook them in boiling water until just tender, then drain. Mix the vinegar and oil in a large bowl with some salt and pepper to make a dressing. Add the hot potatoes and mix gently to coat them in the dressing. Leave until cold, then stir in the mayonnaise and yogurt, soured cream or crème fraîche. Check the seasoning. Sprinkle with chives before serving.

Provençal Puy Lentil Salad Ⓥ

serves 4–6

These little lentils make a delicious salad.

ingredients

225g / 8oz Puy lentils

2 bay leaves

3 or 4 sprigs of thyme

1 onion, finely chopped

2 garlic cloves, crushed

juice of 1 lemon

2 tablespoons balsamic vinegar

4 tablespoons olive oil

salt and freshly ground black pepper

2 tablespoons chopped fresh flat-leaf parsley

Put the lentils into a saucepan with the bay leaves and thyme. Cover generously with water, bring to the boil, then simmer for about 30 minutes or until tender. Drain, and discard the bay leaves and thyme. Add the onion, garlic, lemon juice, balsamic vinegar, olive oil and some salt and pepper to the hot lentils; stir gently then leave until cold. Stir in the chopped parsley before serving.

Sauces and Salsas

A well-chosen sauce can add the perfect finishing touch to a meal from the barbecue. There are plenty of possibilities, many of which can be whizzed up from a **few simple ingredients** with the minimum of cooking. A food processor, or perhaps even better, a hand-held blender, is very useful for making these sauces (and doing a hundred and one other jobs) in a jiffy.

Satay Sauce, and Apricot and Lemon Sauce, page 112, are both examples of this – one based on peanut butter, the other on apricot jam; so too Skordalia, page 109, in which breadcrumbs and garlic are transformed into a **pungent, sensuous cream**. Tahini Cream, page 109, the Pestos, page 108, the Crème Fraîche and Spring Onion Sauce or the Yogurt and

Herb Sauce, both on page 107, and Japanese Dipping Sauce, page 115, are all further, **easy, delectable options.**

Somewhere between a salad, a raw sauce and a dip is a salsa: a mixture of chopped or roughly puréed ingredients, usually raw. The secret of a good salsa is to have a **harmonious balance of flavours** in which you can taste all the ingredients without any one being dominant. A salsa is often made in advance to allow the flavours to develop and mingle. If it contains a large quantity of **green herbs**, it may be best to add these at the last minute, although one favourite of mine, the Coriander Salsa on page 110, contains fresh coriander and parsley which are stirred into the mixture before leaving it to 'mature' for 2–3 hours or overnight. **Richer than a salsa** would be delicious **Pecorino Sauce or Quick Hollandaise Sauce** on page 117: both quick and easy to make.

The recipes which follow can be made ahead of time and with one or two exceptions are served cold. **Lay the sauces and salsas out on a side table for everyone to help themselves immediately they get their food, hot from the grill**.

Crème Fraîche and Spring Onion Sauce

serves 4

This goes well with many dishes as a sauce and makes a good dip for crudités, crisps and tortilla chips. Soured cream can be used instead of crème fraîche.

ingredients

200g / 7oz carton crème fraîche

6 spring onions, trimmed and finely sliced

sea salt and freshly ground black pepper

Put the cream into a bowl with the spring onions, some sea salt and black pepper and mix together.

Yogurt and Herb Sauce

serves 4

This is refreshing and easy to make. Vary the herbs as you wish – mint, chives and dill are all good, as are capers; the mayonnaise version is good too.

ingredients

200g / 7oz carton Greek yogurt

2–3 tablespoons chopped fresh herbs

1 garlic clove, crushed, optional

sea salt and freshly ground black pepper

Mix the yogurt with the herbs and the garlic, if using, then season with sea salt and pepper.

Variations

Yogurt Mayonnaise

Add 2–3 heaped tablespoons good quality bought mayonnaise to the yogurt, garlic (if using) and seasoning; the herbs are optional.

Caper Sauce

Add 2–3 heaped tablespoons good quality mayonnaise and 2 tablespoons drained capers to the yogurt, garlic (if using) and seasoning. The herbs are optional.

Pesto

serves 4

This is the classic pesto made from basil, followed by variations using mint and coriander. It's easy to make a vegan version by simply leaving out the cheese – in this case, make sure it's well-seasoned, perhaps with a dash of chilli powder and salt as well as pepper.

ingredients

2 garlic cloves, crushed

6 tablespoons chopped fresh basil

4 tablespoons chopped fresh flat-leaf parsley

50g / 2oz pine nuts

50g / 2oz freshly grated Parmesan cheese

150ml / 5fl oz olive oil

freshly ground black pepper

Put all the ingredients into a blender or food processor and whiz until smooth.

Variations

Mint Pesto

(V)

Replace the basil and parsley with fresh mint and omit the Parmesan and pine nuts. Add a dash of vinegar and sugar to the seasonings.

Coriander Pesto

Use fresh coriander leaves instead of the basil and parsley, and add a dash of lemon juice to perk up the flavour. The Parmesan is optional.

Red Pepper Pesto

serves 4

Sometimes I make this without the Parmesan and pine nuts and serve it as a sauce.

ingredients

2 red peppers

2 garlic cloves, crushed

50g / 2oz pine nuts

50g / 2oz freshly grated Parmesan cheese

150ml / 5fl oz olive oil

¼ teaspoon chilli powder

sea salt and freshly ground black pepper

Cut the peppers in half and remove the stalk, core and seeds. Put the pepper halves, rounded side up, under the grill and cook for 10–15 minutes until the skin is blistering and black in patches and the flesh is tender. Cool, then remove the outer papery skin. Put the peppers into a food processor with the garlic, nuts, cheese and oil and whiz to a purée. Add the chilli powder and salt and pepper to taste.

Skordalia (V)

serves 4

I've eaten this pungent garlic sauce in various parts of Greece and it has never been quite the same. Sometimes, for example, ground almonds are used in place of some of the breadcrumbs. Whatever its exact composition, it must include plenty of garlic. It goes well with many grilled vegetables. To vary the recipe here, replace half the breadcrumbs with 50g / 2oz ground almonds.

ingredients

6 garlic cloves, crushed to a paste with a little salt

125g / 4oz fresh white breadcrumbs

juice of 1 lemon

sea salt and freshly ground black pepper

4 tablespoons olive oil

Put the garlic, breadcrumbs, lemon juice, a little salt (the garlic already has some) and some pepper into a food processor and blend. Add the olive oil slowly, continuing to blend well, to make a thick pouring consistency. Check the seasoning and serve.

Tahini Cream

serves 4

This has a creamy texture and a slightly bitter flavour. It goes well with grilled dishes that have a Middle-Eastern flavour, such as Aubergine Kebabs, page 45.

ingredients

4 tablespoons pale tahini

2 garlic cloves, crushed

juice of 1 lemon

cold water

salt and freshly ground black pepper

Mix the tahini, garlic and lemon juice then gradually stir in cold water to make the consistency you want. The mixture will go lumpy at first but will become smooth and very creamy as you continue to add liquid and stir. Season with salt and pepper to taste.

Tomato and Ginger Salsa ⓥ

serves 4

I was particularly pleased with the balance of flavours and textures in this salsa; it enlivens many grills.

ingredients

450g / 1lb tomatoes, skinned

½ purple onion

1 garlic clove, crushed

walnut-sized piece of fresh ginger

pinch of cayenne pepper

1 tablespoon caster sugar

3 tablespoons balsamic vinegar

4 tablespoons sultanas

sea salt and freshly ground black pepper

Halve the tomatoes, scoop out and discard the seeds, then finely chop the flesh and put into a bowl. Finely chop the onion and add to the bowl together with the garlic. Wash and coarsely grate the fresh ginger – no need to peel it – and add this to the bowl, along with the cayenne pepper, sugar, balsamic vinegar, sultanas and sea salt and pepper to taste. Leave to stand for at least 30 minutes before serving.

Salsa Verde ⓥ

serves 4

In this version of the classic green sauce, the anchovies are replaced by green olives. Serve it when you want to provide a note of sharp piquancy to cut through the richness of a grilled dish.

ingredients

2 shallots, roughly chopped

1 garlic clove

50g / 2oz best quality green olives, weighed after stoning

2 tablespoons capers

4 tablespoons chopped fresh flat-leaf parsley

3 tablespoons lemon juice

4 tablespoons extra virgin olive oil

Put all the ingredients into a food processor or blender and whiz to a green purée. Serve immediately or keep cool until required.

Coriander Salsa ⓥ

serves 4–6

Make this the night before you want to eat it to allow the flavours to develop fully.

ingredients

225g / 8oz can plum tomatoes in juice

½–1 green chilli, halved, seeded and finely chopped

½ onion, finely chopped

1 small tomato, finely chopped

2 tablespoons finely chopped fresh coriander

2 tablespoons finely chopped fresh flat-leaf parsley

sea salt

Put the tomatoes into a food processor or blender and whiz to a purée. Transfer to a bowl and stir in the remaining ingredients with sea salt to taste. Refrigerate for 2–3 hours or overnight before serving.

Grilled Aubergine Bruschette (page 35), with Coriander Salsa and Barbecue Sauce (page 115)

Apricot and Lemon Sauce (V)

serves 4–6

This sweet sauce is especially good with the Goat's Cheese Burgers or Glamorgan Sausages on pages 75 or 79, or with one of the nut burgers on page 76.

ingredients

350g / 12oz jar apricot jam

grated rind and juice of 1 lemon

Simply spoon the apricot jam into a saucepan with the lemon rind and juice and bring gently to the boil. Serve warm.

Satay Sauce (V)

serves 4

This Asian sauce is particularly good with barbecued tofu (see, for example, page 45), and it also turns a plate of barbecued vegetables into a complete meal.

ingredients

1 rounded tablespoon smooth peanut butter

150ml / 5fl oz water

4 garlic cloves, crushed

50g / 2oz coconut cream or diced creamed coconut

1 tablespoon soy sauce

1 tablespoon medium or sweet sherry

sea salt and freshly ground black pepper

a squeeze of lemon juice

Put the peanut butter, water and garlic into a small saucepan and heat gently to melt the peanut butter. Then add the coconut cream or creamed coconut and stir until melted. Remove from the heat and stir in the soy sauce and sherry with sea salt, pepper and lemon juice to taste.

Red Chilli Sauce (V)

makes 300ml / 10fl oz

This hot dipping sauce is the perfect accompaniment to Thai-flavoured grills. It will keep in the refrigerator for up to 3 weeks. (Illustrated on the facing page.)

ingredients

225g / 8oz large red chillies, halved and seeded

1 shallot, chopped

1 garlic clove, chopped

1 tablespoon light olive oil

50g / 2oz caster sugar

½ teaspoon salt

300ml / 10fl oz water

Par-boil the chillies for 4 minutes. Drain, then put them into a food processor with all the other ingredients apart from the water. Whiz until smooth, then add the water and whiz again. Put the mixture into a saucepan and simmer gently, uncovered, for 45 minutes. Serve at air temperature.

Tomato Sauce

(V)

serves 4

This is good served hot or cold, or as the basis of a spicy Barbecue Sauce, which follows.

ingredients

2 tablespoons olive oil

1 onion, chopped

1 garlic clove, crushed

400g / 14oz can tomatoes in juice, chopped

sea salt and freshly ground black pepper

Heat the oil in a saucepan and add the onion; stir, then cover and cook gently for 7–8 minutes until tender. Stir in the garlic and cook for a minute or two longer. Add the tomatoes with their juice and cook, uncovered, for about 15 minutes, or until the mixture is thick. Season with sea salt and pepper.

Variations

Tomato and Lemon Sauce   **(V)**

Add the grated rind of ½ lemon and 1 tablespoon lemon juice to the mixture along with the sea salt and pepper.

Tomato and Olive Sauce   **(V)**

Add 2 tablespoons chopped black olives to the sauce after cooking. Season only lightly with salt to allow for the sea saltiness of the olives.

Tomato and Green Peppercorn Sauce   **(V)**

Add 1 tablespoonful of brine-preserved green peppercorns, drained, to the cooked sauce.

Tomato and Sun-Dried Tomato Sauce   **(V)**

Drain and chop 8 sun-dried tomatoes and add them to the pan with the canned tomatoes. You could also use the oil in which the sun-dried tomatoes are preserved instead of the olive oil to cook the onion and garlic.

Barbecue Sauce

(V)

serves 4

This is a jazzed up, spicy version of the Tomato Sauce on the facing page; it's delicious with burgers. The quantities of the added ingredients are really a question of personal taste – keep on adding them until it's as you like it.

ingredients

1 quantity of Tomato Sauce, facing page

1 tablespoon tomato ketchup

1 tablespoon soft brown sugar

1 tablespoon soy sauce

1 tablespoon Dijon mustard

dash of balsamic vinegar, optional

sea salt and freshly ground black pepper

Make the tomato sauce as described, then remove from the heat and stir in all the other ingredients. Check the seasoning and serve hot, warm or cold.

Japanese Dipping Sauce (V)

makes 150ml / 5fl oz

This is perfect when you want a light sauce in which to dip grilled vegetables as you eat them. Try it with Baby Aubergines Japanese Style (page 55) and one of the salads on page 96.

ingredients

2 tablespoons caster sugar

4 tablespoons Japanese soy sauce (such as Kikkoman)

6 tablespoons rice vinegar or white wine vinegar

1 tablespoon grated fresh ginger

Mix all the ingredients together well.

Pecorino Sauce

serves 4–6

This sauce adds richness and piquancy to grilled vegetables. It's particularly good with artichokes and asparagus.

ingredients

300ml / 10fl oz medium-sweet white wine

1 teaspoon dried thyme

350g / 12oz strong Pecorino or other firm, sharp-tasting white cheese

450g / 1lb Greek yogurt

sea salt and freshly ground black pepper

Put the wine, thyme and cheese into a saucepan and heat very gently until the cheese has just melted. This takes only a few seconds and it is important not to let the mixture get too hot or you will end up with a sticky mess. As soon as the cheese has melted, remove the pan from the heat and stir in the yogurt. Season with salt and pepper and serve immediately.

Sicilian Artichoke Feast (page 50) with Pecorino Sauce

Quick Hollandaise Sauce

serves 4

Adds richness and piquancy to grilled vegetables ... it's especially good with Grilled Asparagus, page 51. It's best used immediately while it's still warm, although you can make it in advance and reheat it gently by putting it into a bowl over a pan of boiling water. (Illustrated on page 77.)

ingredients

125g / 4oz butter, cut into chunks

2 egg yolks

1 tablespoon freshly squeezed lemon juice

salt and freshly ground black pepper

Melt the butter gently in a saucepan without browning it. Put the egg yolks, lemon juice and some seasoning into a food processor or blender and whiz for 1 minute until thick. With the machine still running, pour in the melted butter in a thin, steady stream, and the sauce will thicken. Leave it to stand for a minute or two, then use immediately while it's still warm or transfer it to a bowl and reheat later as described.

Ices,
Sorbets
and Fruits

Even people who don't
normally care much for
puddings seem to enjoy
eating them out of doors.
   Grilled fruit can make a
pleasant ending to a
barbecued meal, especially
if served with a **creamy
topping**, **ice cream** or a
sorbet. I'd never tried **grilled
fruit** before working on this
book, and I found the results
a **revelation**. The direct heat
on the fruit, undiluted by any
liquid, **brings out its natural
sweetness**, with succulent
results.
   You can, of course, **add
sugar and alcohol** in various

forms to the grilled fruits and top them with sweet or creamy sauces, ices or sorbets. Even if you normally buy these and have never made ice cream before, do try the Quick and Easy Ice Cream, page 120; it really does live up to its name and can be flavoured in exciting ways to enhance whatever you're serving it with.

If you're vegan, or prefer a non-dairy alternative, try the Instant Strawberry Ice Cream, page 121, made with one of the excellent soya 'creams' which you can now buy at health shops and supermarkets (or you can use a soya yogurt). **Yogurt is the basis** for the Cinnamon or Passion Fruit Cream, page 130, which is also delectable with grilled (or fresh) fruits – and there's a vegan version of that, too, based on whipped tofu (much more delicious than it sounds!).

Sorbets are another dairy-free option. **Intensely fruity and utterly refreshing**, they need to be taken out of the freezer a good 30 minutes before you want to eat them. I like to break them up and give them a quick whiz in a food processor just before serving so that they are at their lightest, 'creamiest' and smoothest.

Then there's always **fresh fruit – irresistible when soaked in white wine**, as in the peach recipe on page 127, or served with the minimum of preparation, as in the **jewel-bright** Turkish-Style Iced Fruit Salad, on page 128.

Quick and Easy Ice Cream

serves 8

Whenever I make this ice cream, which is so easy to prepare and has such a velvety texture, I wonder why I ever bother to make ice cream the traditional way with an egg-custard base. This ice cream is superb and can easily be varied in a number of delicious ways.

ingredients

568ml / 1 pint whipping cream

400g / 14oz can sweetened condensed milk

Whisk the cream until thick, then pour in the condensed milk and whisk until the mixture thickens up again.

Pour into a polythene box that fits in the freezer and freeze until firm: this may take 3–4 hours. There is no need to cover the box, and no need to whisk the mixture as it freezes.

Remove the ice cream from the freezer 30 minutes before you serve it.

Variations

Coconut Ice Cream

Luscious with grilled pineapple. Gently stir 6 tablespoons coconut milk powder into the whisked cream and condensed milk.

Ginger Ice Cream

Gently stir in 8 tablespoons chopped preserved ginger and 4 tablespoons syrup to the whisked cream and condensed milk.

Chocolate Ice Cream

'Wickedly delicious' according to my daughter Claire. Stir 200g / 7oz melted plain chocolate into the mixture after adding the condensed milk.

Strawberry Ice Cream

serves 4

A perennial favourite, quick to make and excellent with grilled pears or peaches. Perhaps even nicer made with raspberries – see variation below – although it's more trouble because the raspberries have to be sieved to remove the seeds.

ingredients

**450g / 1lb strawberries,
hulled, roughly sliced**

125g / 4oz caster sugar

juice of ½ lemon

**300ml / 10fl oz double or
whipping cream**

Put the strawberries into a food processor with the sugar and lemon juice and purée. Whisk the cream until it is thick and making floppy peaks. Fold the strawberry purée into the cream. Freeze, in an ice-cream maker according to the manufacturer's instructions, or uncovered in the freezer until firm – take it out about 30 minutes before you want to eat it to allow it to soften a little.

Variation

Raspberry Ice Cream

Replace the strawberries with the same quantity of fresh or frozen raspberries. After puréeing, pass the raspberries through a nylon sieve to remove the seeds.

Instant Strawberry Ice Cream ⓥ

serves 6

This is a delight because you can make it so quickly – without an ice-cream maker. The strawberries need to be well frozen, straight out of the freezer, and you need a food processor strong enough to cope with blending them. You can make the ice cream as high or low fat as you wish, and the vegan version is also excellent.

ingredients

**450g / 1lb frozen strawberries,
straight out of the freezer**

125g / 4oz caster sugar

**568ml / 1 pint single cream,
soya cream or a mixture of
cream and plain natural yogurt**

Pour all the ingredients into a food processor and whiz until thick and creamy – ice cream, in fact. Any left over will keep in the freezer for a short time but it's best eaten immediately.

Pear Sorbet

serves 8

(V)

This is a favourite, especially if laced with Poire Williams liqueur before serving. Wonderful with hot grilled pears.

ingredients

750g / 1½lb ripe dessert pears, peeled, cored and sliced

175g / 6oz caster sugar

1 tablespoon lemon juice

4 tablespoons Poire Williams liqueur, optional

Put the pears into a saucepan with water just to cover, bring to the boil and simmer until tender: 15 minutes or so depending on the size of the pieces. Using a slotted spoon, transfer the pears from the water to a food processor and set aside. Boil the poaching liquid without a lid until it has reduced to 300ml / 10fl oz. Add the sugar and boil for 3–4 minutes. Remove from the heat and cool.

Add the cold sugar syrup to the pears in the food processor, along with the lemon juice, and purée. Pour into a shallow polythene box that will fit into the freezer and freeze until firm.

Remove the sorbet from the freezer 30 minutes before you want to serve it. Just before serving, break it up and put the icy chunks into a food processor – you might need to do this in more than one batch. Whiz at high speed, adding the liqueur if using. The mixture will become pale and fluffy. Serve at once.

Raspberry Sorbet

(V)

serves 6

A wonderful sorbet, well worth the effort of sieving the raspberries. Add the raspberry liqueur – eau de framboises – for a special treat.

ingredients

thinly pared rind and juice of 1 lemon

350g / 12oz caster sugar

400ml / 14fl oz water

700g / 1 1/2 lb raspberries

4 tablespoons *eau de framboises*, optional

Put the lemon rind and juice into a saucepan with the sugar and water. Heat gently until the sugar has dissolved, then increase the heat and boil for 2 minutes. Discard the lemon rind.

Purée the raspberries in a food processor then pass them through a nylon sieve to remove the pips. Mix the raspberry purée with the sugar syrup. Cool, then pour into a shallow polythene box that will fit into the freezer and freeze until firm.

Remove the sorbet from the freezer 30 minutes before you want to serve it. Just before serving, break it up and put the icy chunks into a food processor – you might need to do this in more than one batch. Whiz at high speed, adding the *eau de framboises* if using. The mixture will become pale and fluffy. Serve at once.

Variations

Blackberry or Blackcurrant Sorbet

(V)

Make in exactly the same way, using blackberries or blackcurrants instead of the raspberries. For the special-treat version, add 1 tablespoon port to the blackberry sorbet, and 4 tablespoons *crème de cassis* to the blackcurrant one.

Grilled Chocolate Bananas

serves 6

I first came across the idea for bananas baked in the oven in Marlena Spieler's book of Mexican cookery, and found they also work brilliantly on the barbecue. Serve with vanilla ice cream for an extra treat.

ingredients

4 bananas, slightly under-ripe

150g / 5oz milk chocolate, broken into squares

With a sharp knife make a cut in the top of each banana from end to end, cutting deep into the banana but not going through the skin at the bottom. Open out the slit and pop in the squares of chocolate, dividing them between the four bananas. Wrap the bananas in foil.

TO BARBECUE:
Place the bananas on the grid over medium coals for about 10 minutes, or until the chocolate has melted and the bananas are lightly cooked. Open the foil packages, pull back the banana skin and eat the chocolatey flesh with a teaspoon, with vanilla ice cream if desired.

If not cooked over the barbecue they are probably best done in a moderately hot oven.

Variations

Grilled Ginger Bananas

Stuff each banana with 1 tablespoon chopped stem ginger and a little of the syrup instead of the chocolate.

Grilled Rum Bananas Ⓥ

Stuff each banana with 1 tablespoon dark rum and 2 teaspoons brown sugar instead of the chocolate.

Grilled Chocolate Bananas (top), Grilled Pineapple with Brown Sugar and Rum (bottom)

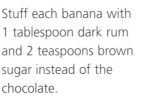

Grilled Pineapple with Brown Sugar and Rum

serves 6

Grilling intensifies the flavour and sweetness of pineapple. Cut into wedges and grill, as here, to serve as an excellent pudding on its own. If you'd like to serve it with a topping or an ice cream – Coconut and Lime Cream Topping, page 130, or Coconut Ice Cream, page 120, are both excellent – peel and core the fruit, slice it into rings and then grill as here.

ingredients

1 large, ripe, juicy pineapple

a little tasteless vegetable oil such as grapeseed

about 6 tablespoons soft brown sugar

6 tablespoons rum

Cut right down through the pineapple, leaves included, slicing it into eighths. Brush both sides of each segment with tasteless vegetable oil.

TO BARBECUE OR GRILL:
Lay the pineapple segments on the barbecue, preferably on a fine-mesh grid, with one cut-side towards the heat. Cook the segments until they are browned underneath, then turn them over, spread with brown sugar and continue to grill until the underneath is browned and the sugar on top has melted. To cook over a hot grill, reverse the procedure: grill one side until browned, turn over and cover the unbrowned side with sugar. Grill until the sugar has melted. Transfer the pineapple to plates and pour the rum over them.

Peaches in White Wine (V)

serves 4–6

A simple recipe that is always popular.

ingredients

6 ripe peaches

300ml / 10fl oz sweet white wine

1–2 tablespoons caster sugar

Skin the peaches by covering them with boiling water, leaving for 1 minute or so until the skins loosen, then draining and removing the skins with a sharp knife. Halve the peaches, discard the stones and cut into thin slices. Put the slices into a serving bowl, cover with the wine and add a little sugar to taste. Chill until required.

Grilled Peaches (V)

serves 4

Warm, grilled peaches are good with Instant Strawberry Ice Cream, page 121, Raspberry Sorbet, page 123, or Butterscotch Sauce, page 131.

ingredients

4 large peaches, not too ripe

a little tasteless vegetable oil such as grapeseed

Cut the peaches in half and remove the stone. Brush lightly with tasteless oil to prevent sticking.

TO BARBECUE OR GRILL: Place cut-side down on a fine-mesh grid over ash-covered coals until tender and lightly browned; turn them over and grill briefly on the other side, then serve. Under a hot grill, cook cut-side up first then reverse to toast the rounded side briefly.

**Grilled Peaches, with
Raspberry Sorbet (page 123)**

Turkish-Style Iced Fruit Salad

(V)

A fruit salad with the minimum of preparation, served in Turkey and throughout the Middle East as a refreshing finale to a meal. How many it serves depends on how much you make. It's especially good accompanied by Yogurt Cinnamon Cream or Passion Fruit Cream, page 130.

ingredients

4 or 5 types of fresh fruit, chosen from watermelon slices, large and luscious strawberries, raspberries, ripe juicy black cherries, grapes, ripe figs, apricots, peaches, nectarines, passion fruit

crushed ice

1 pomegranate, halved, seeds eased out of its skin

wedges of lemon, optional

Prepare the fruit minimally: leave the skin on the watermelon slices, leave the green part on the strawberries; halve or quarter larger fruits such as peaches. Make a bed of crushed ice on a large serving dish, arrange the fruit attractively on top and sprinkle with the pomegranate seeds. Serve at once, with wedges of lemon if desired.

Coconut and Lime Cream Topping (V)

serves 6

A creamy topping perfect for grilled fruits, especially pineapple.

ingredients

125g / 4oz creamed coconut

300ml / 10fl oz water

grated rind and juice of 1 lime

2–3 teaspoons caster sugar

Cut up the coconut cream and put into a small saucepan with the water. Heat gently, stirring, until the creamed coconut has melted. Remove from the heat and cool slightly. Stir in the rind and juice of the lime and sugar to taste. Leave until completely cold. Serve cold but not chilled.

Yogurt Cinnamon Cream

serves 6–8

This can be eaten as a topping spooned over grilled fruit, or as a pudding in itself. The longer in advance it's made, the better – overnight is fine – because the sugar gets deliciously syrupy.

ingredients

300ml / 10fl oz plain natural yogurt

300ml / 10fl oz double cream

½–1 teaspoon ground cinnamon

about 6 tablespoons soft brown sugar

Whisk the yogurt and cream together until thickened and making floppy peaks. Put into a shallow serving dish – a glass one looks attractive – sprinkle the surface lightly with ground cinnamon and then cover it with a thin layer of soft brown sugar. Chill until required.

Variations

Passion Fruit Cream

Omit the cinnamon and the brown sugar. Instead layer the pulp of 6 passion fruit over the whisked yogurt and cream.

Vegan Version

Use the Whipped Tofu Vanilla Topping, page 131, instead of the yogurt and double cream mixture.

Butterscotch Sauce

serves 6

This is sheer indulgence. Pour it over grilled peaches or bananas, or simply over vanilla ice cream.

ingredients

50g / 2oz butter

75g / 3oz soft brown sugar

50g / 2oz caster sugar

2 tablespoons golden syrup

7 tablespoons double cream

few drops of vanilla essence

Heat the butter, sugars and golden syrup in a small saucepan over a low heat until melted, then continue to heat gently for a further 5 minutes. Remove from the heat, transfer to a bowl and allow to cool a little. Then add the cream and vanilla and stir for 2–3 minutes until completely smooth. Serve hot or cold; it will keep for several weeks in a screw-top jar in the refrigerator.

Vegan Variation

Make as described using pure vegetable margarine instead of the butter and soya cream (such as Soya Dream) instead of the double cream.

Whipped Tofu Vanilla Topping

Ⓥ

serves 6

This creamy tofu topping is at its nicest when you purée a whole vanilla pod with the tofu, flecking the mixture with black specks like top quality old-fashioned vanilla ice cream. Alternatively, real vanilla essence can be used.

ingredients

300g / 10oz tofu

honey, sugar or vanilla sugar to taste

½ teaspoon vanilla essence or 1 vanilla pod, broken into pieces

8 tablespoons soya cream such as Soya Dream

Put the tofu into a food processor with a little honey, sugar or vanilla sugar, the vanilla essence or pod and the soya cream. Whiz thoroughly until smooth and creamy. Serve chilled.

Wine, Beer, Cocktails and Aperitifs

Barbecuing is **thirsty work** and the **drinks are as essential** to the success of the occasion as the sunshine and the food. Here are a few thoughts on choosing **wines** and **beers**, followed by a selection of **cocktails**, both alcoholic and non-alcoholic, most of which are the recipes of one of my sons-in-law, Martin, with one or two additions from other friends.

Wines with depth and flavour seem made for barbecued food. On the **red** side, wine made from the **sauvignon grape** is an excellent choice and there are plenty: from France, Australia, South Africa and even Eastern Europe and South America.

I also like a zingy Zinfandel from America, and I'm fond of Italian wines with grilled food; **Salice Salentino, Amarone, Barollo** and of course **Chianti** are all ideal particularly when **tomatoes, mushrooms and cheese** are the main ingredient of the food. On a warm evening, a chilled red wine such as **Beaujolais** or **Brouilly** is always welcome.

As with red wines, among the **whites** there is a great choice. **Chardonnay** is a good choice: an oaky Australian Chardonnay if you want a strong flavour. Two French white wines, both at the top of the price range and both made from the chenin blanc grape – **Mersault, full-bodied, almost oily in texture,** and **Vouvray, a more feminine version and slightly sweeter** – are excellent with **grilled vegetables**; perfect too as an **aperitif**. At the other end of the price range, try Italian whites: **Verdicchio, Orvieto** and **Corvo Bianco.**

Or you could opt for a **chilled rosé.** It's a lovely, summery choice, ideal for drinking outside and to me always brings **a celebratory feeling to an occasion.**

As for beer, even those who prefer real ale agree nothing is more refreshing than well-chilled lager with barbecued food. Choose a good quality **full-bodied lager**, though not necessarily one of the most expensive brands. To ensure enough **flavour and bite**, lager usually needs to be about 5 per cent alcohol by volume.

Excellent beers and lagers at competitive prices, including bottled, own-brand lagers from Germany, Spain, Alsace and Australia, are readily available in supermarkets and off-licences. Martin particularly enjoys **Sainsbury's Spanish Cerveza**, which has a **strong and rustic flavour**, and also **Mexican beers**, with the obligatory **wedge of lime** pushed through the neck of the bottle into the beer for ease of drinking. He says **Swan Light** is the only low-alcohol or **alcohol-free lager** worth drinking.

If you're a real-ale fan you'll know your favourites. A few that have been recommended to me are **Tesco's Strong Yorkshire Bitter** – smooth and excellent value; **Gales HSB** – wonderful beer with a hint of caramel; **Shepherd Neame's Spitfire** – splendid; **Fuller's London Pride** and **Wadworth's 6X** – excellent traditional ales; **Morland's Old Speckled Hen** and **Hall and Woodhouse's Tanglefoot** – best lightly chilled; and **Hook Norton's Old Hooky.**

Cocktails and Aperitifs

Here is a selection of cocktails and aperitifs, including some that are alcohol-free. It's probably most practical to choose two or three and make them up in quantity rather than individually. Make sure you have plenty of ice available; buying it from a supermarket saves time.

Unless otherwise stated, all these cocktails serve one; a measure is 25ml (just under 1fl oz).

Mai Tai – Original or Fruity (V)

Invented in California in the 1940s, Mai Tai has a Polynesian feel and if you've been to Hawaii it evokes instant memories.

ingredients

1 measure white rum

1 measure dark rum

⅔ measure triple sec (or Cointreau)

⅓ measure almond syrup or a drop of almond essence

½ teaspoon caster sugar, optional

¼ measure grenadine

juice of 1 lime

Mix everything together and add to a glass of ice cubes; or add to crushed ice and serve with a straw.

The fruity version, which is wonderful, is made as above but with the addition of 3 measures fresh pineapple juice and 3 measures fresh orange juice.

Pimm's No. 1 (V)

enough for 10

Perfect for large parties.

ingredients

700ml / 24fl oz Pimm's No. 1

2 litres / 3½ pints fresh lemonade

2 sprigs of fresh borage (if unavailable, use fresh mint)

slices of red delicious apple, orange, lemon, cucumber

Mix the Pimm's and lemonade in a punch bowl with ice and add the borage and sliced fruit. Dangerously drinkable.

Cuba Libre (V)

A classic, originating from Cuba at the end of the last century following the arrival of Coca-Cola. Traditionally Bacardi is used, but you can use any white rum.

ingredients

2 measures white rum

5 measures cold cola

juice of half a lime

Mix together and place in a glass with ice and the squeezed-out half lime.

Bawdy Bloody Mary (V)

serves 8

My friend Joseph Michenfelder's Bloody Marys – the best I have ever tasted – are famous in Brooklyn. Brunch on Sunday morning begins with Bawdy Bloody Marys and continues throughout the day. Here is his recipe, exactly as he faxed it to me from New York. Joe says, 'Serve Bawdy Bloody Marys with a selection of hard cheeses, Brie and wafers, and a cold fresh veggie selection of carrots, cucumbers, green peppers and pitted sexy black olives. The recipe uses American quarts: for 2 US quarts use 2 litres or 3½ pints. A jigger is 1½fl oz, or about 40ml.

ingredients

2 quarts V8 (or tomato) juice, chilled (see note above)

juice of 1 lemon

1 tablespoon Worcestershire sauce

1 teaspoon Tabasco

2 tablespoons grated fresh red or white horseradish

8 jiggers of Gilbey's vodka (see note above)

freshly ground black pepper

8 stalks of ice-crisp celery

Mix the ingredients, except the pepper and celery, in a glass pitcher, stirring with a bit of vigour. Pour over roughly chipped ice in tall glasses, add the black pepper and garnish (as bawdily as possible) with celery stalks, one to a glass. (See the note about Worcestershire sauce on the right, in the recipe for Virgin Bloody Mary.)

Virgin Bloody Mary (V)

serves 6

As the name suggests!

ingredients

5 measures tomato juice

¼ measure lemon juice

4 drops Tabasco sauce

pinch each of salt and freshly ground black pepper

Mix and serve with or without ice. Traditionally a Bloody Mary uses Worcestershire sauce, most brands of which contain anchovies. Although a vegetarian version is available, it's not always easy to find, but here I have successfully omitted it without detriment to the flavour. However, if you can get a variety without anchovies, add a couple of drops to taste.

Daiquiri – Original, on the Rocks and Frozen

(V)

Another delicious cocktail originating in Cuba at the end of the last century near the town of Daiquiri.

ingredients

1 teaspoon caster sugar, optional

2 measures white rum

⅔ measure lime juice

slice of lime, to decorate

Use the sugar to coat the rim of a chilled glass, if desired. Mix the rum and lime juice and serve in the chilled glass. Serve over ice for a Daiquiri on the rocks, or whiz in a blender with a glassful of ice for a frozen version. Decorate with a slice of lime.

Daiquiri, like margarita, can be transformed into a fruit version. Again, do experiment; below is a peach Daiquiri as an example but excellent variations include strawberry and raspberry.

Virgin Raspberry Daiquiri

(V)

Like the other non-alcoholic drinks here, this looks and tastes great and is perfect for those who want a cocktail but who are not drinking alcohol. (Illustrated on page 139.)

ingredients

3 measures raspberry purée

2 measures pineapple juice

½ measure lemon juice

½ measure raspberry syrup

mint sprigs and strawberries or raspberries, to decorate

Blend together with a glassful of crushed ice and decorate with a sprig of fresh mint and fresh raspberries or strawberries.

Peach Daiquiri

(V)

ingredients

1½ measures white rum

1 measure peach schnapps

⅓ peeled, stoned, ripe peach (or nectarine)

½ teaspoon caster sugar, optional

¾ measure lime juice

slice of peach, to decorate

Whiz the ingredients together in a blender with a glassful of ice until smooth. Decorate with a slice of peach and serve with a straw.

Margarita –
on the Rocks or Frozen

serves 6

A perfect cocktail for barbecues on a hot summer's day. First drunk in Tijuana, Mexico, in 1948, it is traditionally made with silver tequila but is also excellent with gold; I prefer it made with the gold.

ingredients

2 measures tequila

1¼ measures triple sec (or Cointreau)

¾ measure lemon juice

salt and lemon, to coat the glass

wedge of lemon, to decorate

Mix the tequila, sec and lemon juice. For a margarita on the rocks, rim the glass with lemon juice and salt, serve the drink over ice cubes in the glass and garnish with a wedge of lemon. For a frozen version whiz the margarita with ice in a blender and serve in a glass with a straw.

Frozen margaritas can be transformed into delicious fruit versions by the addition of fresh fruit and an appropriate fruit liqueur. See the recipe that follows, and don't be afraid to try out your own ideas.

Frozen Peach Margarita

ingredients

1 measure tequila

1 measure peach schnapps

½ measure triple sec (or Cointreau)

⅓ peeled, stoned, ripe peach or nectarine

¾ measure lemon juice

slice of peach, to decorate

Whiz the ingredients with a glassful of ice in a blender. Serve garnished with a slice of peach.

Virgin Raspberry Daiquiri (page 137) and Margarita on the Rocks

Cinderella (V)

ingredients

2 measures fresh orange juice

2 measures fresh pineapple juice

1 measure lemon juice

½ teaspoon caster sugar

1 measure soda water or sparkling mineral water

A refreshing, sparkling, non-alcoholic drink.

Mix and serve on the rocks.

Fruit Cocktail (V)

serves 4

The following is a really tasty but simple non-alcoholic fruit cocktail.

ingredients

300 ml/10 fl oz fresh orange juice

300 ml/10 fl oz fresh grapefruit juice

½ really ripe pineapple, peeled, cored and puréed in a blender

Mix together and cool in the refrigerator or serve with ice.

Index

Index